I0521083

Praise for Indra's Net

Recipient of the **Literary Titan Gold Book Award** in Nonfiction

Adult Nonfiction Book of the Year, San Francisco Writer's Conference

"Reading the book, I kept feeling a mix of surprise and comfort… the ideas stirred up a strange mix of awe and restlessness… that emotional tug made the book stick with me… the book feels authentic, and that gave it a texture that pulled me deeper… it all creates a rhythm that feels like a long walk with someone who has been on the road a while and wants you to see the scenery with fresh eyes… it is especially good for people who want a companion on their inward journey."
- **Literary Titan**

"Rinzler's perspectives on life are certainly unique–and entertaining! He does a great job mixing sincerity with humor, offering uplifting advice while never negating the harder parts of life too… I like the expansiveness of Rinzler's approach, focusing on subtle inward transformation that ripples outward to have major effects. There's a gentleness to each thematic entry that encourages meaningful contemplation rather than intense action… So many life lessons packed into this text!"
- **Alanna Kali, Discovery**

"This is a five-star resource that has earned a permanent place on my desk. Whether used for daily inspiration, deeper study, or as a guide to mindful living, it consistently offers clarity and a sense of cosmic connection. Highly recommended for any seeker looking to make sense of the human experience with more wisdom and heart."
- **Tricia Livingston, Goodreads review**

"The text offers you rich perspectives and insights that can shift your worldview and open your consciousness to a deeper understanding of yourself and how your unique soul fits into and is amplified by Indra's Net."
- **Julie Hilsen, Author of** *Life of Love: A Joyful Guide to Self and Sensuality*

"*Indra's Net* is one of those rare books that feels like a companion for the soul… a guide that is both deeply awakening and profoundly practical…Rinzler doesn't preach—he invites. With gentleness and clarity, he helps readers see themselves more honestly and compassionately."
- **Angelina Carleton, Design Your Legacy-Live Lessons Podcast**

"If you've grown weary of spiritual self-help, this book demands a reckoning… The themes in this book will help you to awaken to your true essential Self."
- **Stephen Sturgess, Kriya Yoga Meditation Teacher, Author, and Artist**

"Indra's Net brings us the teachings of the ages into a modern context and offers guidance and answers that can free us from the limitations of the mind."
- **Arielle Guttman, Author & Astrologer**

"Super cool book."
- **Laurie Haas Young, Long-time Tarot Card Reader**

"Blending mysticism, autobiography, and symbolic instruction, Rinzler presents intuition as a primary organizing principle of life. Through striking metaphor, he teaches that all existence is interconnected and reflects divine intelligence, building the guide's ideas around the Tarot structure to provide a concrete framework for those abstract spiritual concepts. The book's themes move from ordinary life situations into profound awareness, encouraging change through reflection and hands-on experience."
- **BookLife Reviews**

"In a world that often prioritizes fragmentation over wholeness, Indra Rinzler's *Indra's Net* arrives not merely as a book, but as a profound invitation to remember our place in the grand tapestry of existence. This is a work of immense generosity, distilling timeless wisdom from many paths into a format that is both profoundly deep and eminently practical. For any seeker of answers, understanding, or inner peace, this book is not just a five-star read, it is a lifelong companion and a beacon of transformative light."
- **Stephen Jay, Goodreads Review**

"As someone familiar with Tarot, I found *Indra's Net* to be a refreshing and expansive reimagining of the tradition. While honoring the structure of a Tarot deck, the book transcends conventional meanings and opens the door to a more personal and intuitive form of spiritual discovery. The reflections feel alive, insightful, and accessible, making the book both a learning tool and a meditative companion. It deepened my understanding of interconnection and reminded me that Tarot and life itself are less about prediction and more about awareness, presence, and choice."
- **Sarah M., Goodreads Review**

"*Indra's Net* is a beautifully layered and deeply contemplative guide for anyone walking a spiritual path. Indra Rinzler weaves wisdom, compassion, and lived experience into reflections that feel both ancient and strikingly relevant. Each theme invites the reader inward, encouraging a gentler, more honest relationship with the Self and the world."
- **John Steward, Goodreads Review**

"This book has become part of my daily spiritual practice. Each entry in *Indra's Net* offers something meaningful to sit with, whether it's a reminder about impermanence, gratitude, or vulnerability. The writing is thoughtful, warm, and quietly transformative. The book never feels heavy or preachy. It feels like guidance offered with humility and love. It's a source of inspiration that continues to reveal new insights with each return."
- **Jacob Levine, Goodreads review**

INDRA'S NET

A SEEKER'S Guide to the Human Experience

INDRA RINZLER

Moving Beyond

Copyright @ 2025 by R. Indra Rinzler

Published by Moving Beyond

ISBN: 979-8-9999831-0-7

Printed in the United States of America

10 9 8 7 6 5 4 3 2 1

First Edition Printing

Editing & Design by Krista Huber of West Beach Publishing. Contact at www.westbeachpublishing.com

Original Cover Art by Jennifer Michelle McEuen. Readers can learn more about Jennifer's art at jennifermichellemceuen.com

Illustration of Mahavatar Babaji (page 146) by Stephen Sturgess (London, UK)

Photographs on pages 192 & 220 are by Indra Rinzler

All other images in the book were carefully selected and intentionally chosen from online stock programs, from which rights were also purchased.

Dedicated to a lifetime of teachers, with deep love and appreciation.

INDRA'S NET

A NOTE TO THE READER

Language is layered. A single word can have multiple meanings, uses, and/or intonations. Written language is even more difficult because it lacks the tonal nuances of spoken language. Because of this, I'd like to orient you to my use of language in this book.

Throughout *Indra's Net*, I will be using terms that, depending on how they are written, will have one of three different meanings. The terms to notice are "self," "knowing," and "truth". Here is a guide to those layers.

self/knowing/truth (uncapitalized noun): This is the lower self. The one that acts out, live unconsciously, gets stuck in past and future, runs continual mental stories, and can't access intuition and the like.

Self/Knowing/Truth (capitalized proper noun): This is the Highest Self and internal Divine Knowing. This refers to Divinity itself—God, Enlightened Beings, individuals living beyond a sense of self and beyond agenda, expectations, and even the need for freedom.

self/knowing/truth (uncapitalized noun; italic): There is a third category, somewhere in between the lower self and Highest Self. This self/knowing/truth is conscious, acts with ethics, is sincerely nice and open to people, and acts with wisdom, but it is not coming from Divinity. This *self/knowing/truth* lives with intuition, mostly in the present, and can release compulsions of the mind.

Understanding these variations will add to your growth and clarity as a reader. I believe that as you bring these definitions into your personal life, you will gain clarity from seeing how these words operate for you in each moment.

In addition, there are some other special words that are synonymous with the goals of the spiritual path, which can be written with capitals as a full expression of Divinity. Many times, I will use them uncapitalized because generally we are not on the highest levels in our experience of them. These words include: presence, existence, consciousness, nothingness, emptiness, awareness, awakening, enlightenment, and spirit.

INTRODUCTION

The Author

What you are holding in your hands is the book I always wanted to write. The desire to write a book has been with me for my entire life, but of course, I had doubts that it would happen. I am proud to be associated with *Indra's Net*. I hope this book will be a friend you'll want to spend time with. What came through was powerful for me, and I hope it is for you, too.

I've been on the spiritual path since 1971. Early on, I became a disciple of Paramahansa Yogananda, author of the classic spiritual book *Autobiography of a Yogi*. I lived in a spiritual community for twenty years, where I raised a family and learned about discipleship and the spiritual path.

Starting in 1999, and for the next twenty years, I traveled the world, spending winters in India sitting with many teachers and intensely reading about spiritual paths and teachings. Ideas and philosophies from Hinduism, Buddhism, and non-duality have become part of my deeper understanding of spirituality alongside my own reflections.

As part of my current work, I offer personal reading sessions using my unique approach, which combines Vedic astrology, the Enneagram of Personality, location astrology, and intuition. The readings provide insights that help clients live in their higher selves by waking up to who they really are, not who they *think* they are, the small self.

This book makes the services I offer to individual clients available to potential readers all over the world, helping them ground themselves and live in their higher *selves* through its teachings.

Indra's Net is assembled from the decades of study, wisdom paths, practices, and experiences. Some wisdom and insights present in this manuscript are certainly from a higher source. I have felt the gentle guiding hand of a muse or spirit guide, whose whispers into presence appear to me through *knowing* (2 The Yogini). I receive guidance about words and ideas, kind of like puzzle parts, that need to be assembled to comprehend the total picture.

It is only now, at a mature age in years, that intuition is strong enough to physically feel the presence that encourages. I feel fine with the truth that the cosmic intelligence in this book appeared more *through* me than from me.

The alignment of all makes it clear. It is my time to communicate and share. This is my way of showing up for the larger pulls of the Universe that invite us into deeper versions of ourselves for the benefit of everyone. I am very honored to share *Indra's Net* with you.

What is Indra's Net

Indra's Net is a collection of themes about learning to live an awakened life and opening one's mind and heart to the *self.*

At its most basic, it is a book of carefully crafted short stories that provide unique, entertaining perspectives on life's experiences.

Inside the book, one will find inspiration through many teachers and paths, cultural and spiritual symbols, personal experiences and revelations, and insights that appeared to me while working with clients all over the world for the last ten years.

On a larger scale, the book is a product of over fifty years of living as a seeker on the spiritual path and learning through surrender to the higher Self to navigate life. It covers subjects broadly and deeply. Everything becomes a symbol.

Indra's Net is for those who seek answers, understanding, inspiration, and inner peace. When we deepen our vision, the answers often appear. The parables contained within this book are intended to aid in that deepening. The book provides a transcendental experience at a higher frequency. The totality of what the book is and will be has yet to be determined.

We will look at hard topics like vulnerability, codependence, arrogance, impermanence, gratitude, and failure. We will be inspired by wisdom and teachers from many paths.

Indra's Net is full of helpful techniques, hints, humor, and love, all oriented towards making sense of our human experiences and discovering a cosmic home here on Earth.

While unique in focus, the themes have a common purpose: helping us wake up to our truest Self. The primary messages are repeated over and over: live in your heart, live in the moment, release anything you hold.

Indra's Net is a *how to do* and *how to be* manual. It's an almanac that will meet you where you are, without judgment.

It's also an adventure. The themes are literal, yet rich with allegory and symbolism. They are meant to entertain and then, through inspiration, effortlessly transform the reader. *Indra's Net* is a book of stretching exercises meant to raise vibrations. The version of you that starts reading the book won't be the same as the version at the end.

This book can be used as daily inspiration, a tool for self-improvement, a spiritual lesson plan, and a source of divination.

2

How we view life is our choice. This book is meant to encourage you to choose from a higher wisdom and connection to the truest Self. That which we wish to understand and become, transforms us in the very process of seeking. As we open to awareness, we awaken to the significance of all dimensions of reality.

How the Book is Organized

This book is divided into 78 themes—each with unique expressions, contemplations, and guidance. Themes are slices of life.

The format mirrors a traditional Tarot card deck. However, themes are not intended to represent the traditional meanings of Tarot cards, though they do match the esoteric, energetic frequency of them. The Tarot organization gives the themes a framework and structure within which to exist. Together, they shine light on new meanings in the themes and cards, expanding the possibilities.

I like to say that placing the themes into the Tarot format is like pouring batter into a muffin tin. The Tarot gives the wisdom in this book a recognizable shape. For deeper information, there is a section titled "The Tarot" later in the introduction that further explains the relationship between Tarot and *Indra's Net*.

I have worked with divination tools my whole life and, in particular, Tarot, for more than twenty-five years. These tools are somehow able to highlight accurate answers to our deepest questions by focusing us on dimensions beyond our grasp.

There are three sections in the book:

The Major Truths

The Major Truths are the first twenty-two themes (in descending order) that embody heavier topics such as accessing your inner knowing, self-worth, and cosmic intelligence. These themes help readers understand the broad spiritual context and then guide them through tests towards living in freedom.

The Teachers

The next section is The Teachers—Living, Loving, Releasing, and Observing. Each teacher contains four themes, one in each of the four suits (explained below), for a total of sixteen. These themes are about learning to live in the moment and love oneself. They encourage the reader to observe their own thinking and behavior objectively, as well as their reactions to other people's thinking and behavior, and then let go of what doesn't serve them.

3

The Minor Truths

The final section contains The Minor Truths. These last forty themes are divided into four "suits"—Energy, Flow, Intelligence, and Gravity. Each suit contains ten themes, numbered from Ace-10, like a standard deck of playing cards. In this section, each theme has its own flavor, sharing challenges and opportunities that come to us through the ebb and flow of daily life.

Energy (fire) is grounded, direct, and clear. It helps us examine feelings that become motivated into action.

Flow (water) is about discovering our intuition. Flow involves emotions, so it can be slippery and harder to grasp.

Intelligence (air) is airy and amorphous. It needs focus and requires an analytical intelligence, challenging us to understand reality on deep levels.

Gravity (earth) is fun, straightforward, and very grounding. It investigates the physical world and our perceptions of our place within it.

In addition to the organization explained above, there are many other levels from which the reader can see, understand, and interpret the themes.

Visuals as a metaphor

In addition to the written content, the images at the start of each theme offer a broader, more metaphorical interpretation of each theme, while layering context and expanding possibilities.

Progression within themes

Each theme begins grounded in an experience of the external world and progresses to a spiritual teaching.

Polarity within themes

Each theme contains a polarity from the highest (bliss and joy) to the lowest (pain and suffering), and everything in between.

Now and later

The end of each theme offers suggestions for immediate shifts to use after reading the theme, as well as actions that can deepen over time with greater use.

Progression of themes

The themes move in a flow, or cadence, that embodies many levels of understanding and appreciation. In individual themes and from theme to theme, we experience from heaviest to lightest and from ethereal and intangible to grounded and clear.

Tarot organization

Though the book does not subscribe to the strict hierarchy of the Tarot, one could easily utilize the levels of the Tarot when interpreting the book's themes.

Journey on a spiritual path

From beginning to end, and onward, the book can be used as a kind of guide on a spiritual path. It can serve this way if read in order from beginning to end, or if taken at random based on the intuition of the reader and guidance of the Universe.

How to Read This Book

Though the themes are particularly ordered, as the reader, you get to choose how to read them. You can read the book cover-to-cover, open it up and pick a theme to read, flip through the pages and stop where you feel called, or pick a card from a Tarot deck and compare it to the corresponding card in this book using the comparison chart at the end of this introduction. You can also ask a question before choosing a tarot card or flipping to a theme.

It's all the same. It's all a message. And the best way to discover the message is by using your intuition. Move around the book however feels right to you.

Each theme has a set design layout, composed of nine separate elements, which look like this:

Image: Each card begins with an image. The photos are intended to make the message more visible and add more dimensions to the offering. Each has a caption-like statement underneath the photo. These statements are reflections on the photo AND the theme. It is offered as a way to begin approaching an understanding of the theme's meaning.

Experience: This is the story of the theme. The stories have a rhythm to them, building up from mundane to spiritual, from challenges to solutions, and from general, physical life examples to specific lessons.

Significance: In alignment with traditional Tarot cards, about twelve subjects are listed in association with each theme. These keywords are used to help focus the energy of the theme.

5

Lessons: The lessons combine the theme and the subject of its associated Tarot card to offer a more clearly defined interpretive answer.

Practices: These are exercises designed to deepen the subject and open the reader to further understanding through their own experience.

Next Step: A suggested next step to take on the spiritual path.

Contemplate: A meditation to deepen the understanding of the subject.

Higher Octave: A view of the theme from a higher peak.

Affirmation: Last words of advice or encouragement that have a way of cutting through all misunderstandings. These can be said aloud by the reader as affirmations or chanted during meditation as often as needed.

Leveling Up

One of the unique aspects of *Indra's Net* is the idea of "leveling up." As explained above, for each card, there are various components. The last seven—Significance, Lessons, Practices, Next Step, Contemplate, Higher Octave, and Affirmation—offer additional, simplified meanings for the reader. They provide possibilities for actions and next steps based on the reader's truth.

They provide direction and focus without prophecy and prediction.

By opening ourselves to being changed, that which we seek to understand changes us. These points allow the reader to expand their understanding and grow.

Spiritual development and evolution are facilitated by understanding and opening to consciousness itself. It is a process of relinquishing anything that isn't peace, viewing challenges as helping us reach higher and deeper, surrendering the idea of control, and believing that we are doing the best we can at all times. This is the process of "leveling up."

The Tradition

Indra's Net is a mystical symbol that comes to us from the ancient Vedic times in India, and is found in Buddhist, Hindu, and non-duality traditions.

Though different versions exist around the world, the concept is generally understood as follows.

Indra was the King of the Gods, and he had a net. That net was big enough to cover the entire Universe. A perfect faceted jewel hung at each crossing point in the net, and each jewel reflected every other jewel.

The net with its jewels is an image of interdependence. Everything is connected to everything else. Indra's Net is not only a poetic philosophical idea, but also the way life functions. When we are true to the Self, and we live this way, connected to everything else, we shine. Our brightness dims when we believe in ideas of separation.

The net, in its largest sense, symbolizes consciousness. Together with Tarot, *Indra's Net*, the book, indicates how consciousness works and thus guides our souls to understand human experiences.

The themes within this book are like Indra's Net—they are interconnected. Everything reflects everything else; everything is connected; all is one. The Tarot is an example of Indra's Net, as is the internet.

The Bhagavad Gita is a respected Hindu scripture that is at least 2,000 years old. In it, the God Krishna says, "There is no power in the cosmos that does not emanate from Me and belong to Me. The entire universe is suspended from Me as if I were the string in a necklace of jewels. The gems may differ vastly, but the force holding them all together, the central thread is Me, Divinity."

The title also has another meaning. Indra is a spiritual name given to the author nearly thirty years ago, and so this book is this Indra's Net too. It contains my stories, experiences, and wisdom, serving as a type of memoir—a personal journal that provides an inward call to assess *How do I want to live*?

The Tarot

Indra's Net is a collection of parables in Tarot form.

For readers who are not already versed in the Tarot and who are interested in learning more about the connection between the Tarot and *Indra's Net*, there is much more to be understood.

Although the exact origins of the Tarot are unknown, we do know that there is a record of them being used as a fortune-telling tool as early as the 1400s in Italy. It has grown in popularity over the last two centuries, but has undergone an explosion in popularity in the last fifty years.

In the most popular standard modern deck, there are 78 illustrated cards divided into two groups: 22 major arcana, which are also known as trumps, and 56 minor arcana, which are divided into four suits of 14 cards each. The suits are wands, cups, swords, and pentacles, each containing a court (King, Queen, Knight, and Jack) and numbered cards

7

Ace-10, the same as a standard deck of playing cards.

The major arcana generally represents larger spiritual matters, and the minor arcana represent career/business (wands), love (cups), conflict (swords), and money/material comfort (pentacles). Each of the 78 cards in the deck has a unique metaphorical meaning assigned to it.

There are usually two users: a questioner and a fortune-teller, now commonly called a reader. First, the deck is shuffled by the questioner while he or she quietly focuses on the question they want to ask. Then, the reader lays out a certain number of cards in a spread. There are various versions of popular spreads, depending on the reader's preference. Finally, the reader reads the cards in the order determined by the spread and uses the metaphorical meanings of each card to ascertain an answer to the questioner's queries.

It is generally understood that there is a particular hierarchy assigned to the cards, with some more important than others. Trumps "beat" the minor arcana, and the numerically "higher" minor arcana "beat" the "lower" ones.

There is also a good/bad value assigned to certain cards or instances of the cards. For example, the ten of swords is commonly understood to represent complete ruin. Furthermore, a card that lands upside down in the spread is often read by readers as having a negative version or reversed meaning of the intended meaning of the card.

There are countless books on the history, development, and philosophy of the Tarot, and I encourage you to read further if this is a topic that interests you.

The Tarot and Indra's Net

There is also an abundance of books that offer new, revised, or expanded meanings of the 78 cards. It is a popular practice to use these more modern books to expand one's understanding of the cards and to elaborate on the reading of the spread.

If one is so inclined, *Indra's Net* can be used in this exact way. However, though this book complements and honors the Tarot tradition, there are some aspects of the Tarot to which *Indra's Net* does not subscribe.

No themes/cards "beat" any others. There is no hierarchical meaning to this collection of themes. Instead, each theme/card is like a jewel in Indra's Net—each of equal importance, and each with a meaning from which to learn. Here, there is Divine in everything, and the story flows like in astrology—house to house, sign to sign. None is greater than any other. The rhythm is your own.

No cards have a "good" or "bad" meaning. Each theme contains a polarity from the highest (bliss and joy) to the lowest (pain and suffering). Ultimately, however, each one is no different from the other.

And although the themes in *Indra's Net* draw on the wisdom of the Tarot, this is not a guide to the Tarot. Instead, it's an application of the Tarot as a way to explore wisdom and self. The cards aren't meant to do our work. They highlight areas of significance and allow the reader to interpret further.

The final way in which this book differs from the traditional Tarot deck is in the order of the first 22 themes, the Major Truths. Instead of being listed 0-21, they are listed in reverse order from 21-0. I call this the twist.

There are a few reasons for this twist. I enjoy the way they build upon each other in this order. It is also a challenge to traditional and forward ways of thinking that keep our minds closed to our conditioned behaviors. The twist has a fresh new beginning and a contemporary, or maybe even futuristic, way about it. Finally, the reverse order helps break down patriarchal archetypal ways of thinking and being—ideas of supreme rulers and life based on seeking and valuing material success. It drops all the conditioning in a simple move. I live to unwind that kind of thinking and structure.

I saw the twist as a coming home—an unwinding from the old end card to the old beginning card, as we go forward in backward order. Thus, *Indra's Net*'s Tarot became the Tarot of Coming Home and a catalyst for change.

Pulling Cards

If you want to pull cards alongside this book, you can pull a card from any Tarot deck and then read the associated theme in this book as additional information and context for your card.

I suggest pulling one card and reading one theme for each question. To me, a spread feels like too much information.

Your question can be specific or general. I do not suggest asking "when" questions. If you don't know what to ask, it is fine to simply ask, *What do I need to learn*? Or, *What's my next step*?

Ideally, you always have someone else pulling your card for you, as your emotions and ego can affect the answers you get when you pull your own card.

If you do pick your own card, try to let go of expectation. Pick a card randomly, without ceremony, but with intention.

Table of Contents & Comparisson to Classic Tarot Deck

The Waite Deck is the most popular mainstream Tarot deck by A.E. Waite and Pamela Colman Smith, first produced in 1909.

Note: The cards are listed in order of the themes in Indra's Net. Traditionally, the Waite deck starts with 0 The Fool and moves in ascending numerical order.

THE MAJOR TRUTHS

21 - THE UNIVERSE

In a VERY quick moment, everything was changed.
Life as we know it was begun for this cycle.
The big bang was just the first miracle.
Life is a series of miracles, moment to moment.

Experience: The Universe

In his book, A Brief History of Time, written 40-some years ago, Stephen Hawkins explains the beginning of the existence of our universe. He says:

"We can explain why the big bang occurred about ten thousand million years ago—it takes about that long for intelligent beings to evolve. An early generation of stars had to form. These stars converted some of the original hydrogen and helium into elements like carbon and oxygen, out of which we are made. The stars then exploded as supernovas, and their debris went to form other stars and planets, among them those of our solar system, which is about five thousand million years old. The first one or two thousand million years of the earth's existence were too hot for the development of anything complicated. The remaining three thousand million years or so have been taken up by the slow process of biological evolution, which has led them from the simplest organisms to beings who are capable of measuring time back to the big bang."

It took 10 billion years and somehow, he condenses those years down to just a few simple acts—keystrokes of moments in time. The basis is high school science. Elements get changed into other elements; heat is involved.

I am impressed by how the cosmic intelligence takes care of us. It is kind of like my wife's cooking: a tomato there, a spice here, a little time, and wow, what a meal.

A few days ago, I read an online comment about how there isn't any food delivery except for pizza in my hometown in California. A user wrote that if he wants some Chinese food, "Oh well, I guess I have to go get it myself." Maybe this is an understandable complaint, but come on guys, get some perspective.

It took two billion years just to cool the planet down to livable temperatures! Let's broaden our viewpoint a bit. Let's live like this life is a miracle, which in fact it is.

I wake up in the morning. Wake up from what to what? I get hungry. What is hunger? I eat my oatmeal. It tastes so good. What is taste? How do I know what it tastes like? It digests and feeds my body. How many cells are involved, how many chemical reactions have occurred? I notice but I don't do anything; It just happens on its own.

And yet we live like life owes us what we want right here, right now.

The periodic table of elements isn't just a list of elements. It explains the alchemical-like experience of you! Take an element, add a neutron or proton and poof! It is an entirely different element. When we don't see the deep implications these simple facts have for us, it's easy to disrespect our neighbors simply because they are different from us.

There is awe in the complete and total miracle of life. Food grows, we eat. It is digested and the body keeps functioning. We get a fresh reset each day. Our daily reset is like the ten-billion-year condensation of a living organism, Universe, that reminds us of a presence at work in our life. Let each day become like a big bang to show us the miracle that life is in the Universe.

Significance: Saturn, focus, discipline, restriction, construction, seriousness, details, completion, releasing old karma, self-knowledge, wheel of life, unification, responsibility

Lessons: The most basic lesson of life applies here: As above, so below. The completion of life's cycle is to see the large and the small as the same. Make all events in life in harmony with the Universe, life happens for us, not to us. The simplest of truths, like how ants support each other, can be the key to opening to the highest joy.

Practices: Actively feel gratitude for everything that comes in a day. Find a place where you can observe insects working. Make friends with some restrictions you have met in your life.

Next Step: Work on trusting and accepting what is instead of asking for more.

Contemplate: All the bodily and natural functions that happen on their own without you having to think about it or do anything.

Higher Octave: Freedom from burdensome responsibility. We make responsibility burdensome.

Affirmation: The Universe and I are one.

20 – THE STATESMAN ELDER

Mātā Amritānandamayī Devi, known to the world as Amma, the "hugging" saint, has been circling the world for over thirty years as a guru and humanitarian, literally hugging millions of people one at a time.
Her organization focuses on providing the poor with our five basic needs: food, shelter, healthcare, education, and livelihood.
Regarding her desire to embrace others, Amma commented,
"I don't see if it is a man or a woman. I don't see anyone different from my own self. A continuous stream of love flows from me to all of creation. This is my inborn nature. The duty of a doctor is to treat patients. In the same way, my duty is to console those who are suffering."

Experience: Isn't it Wonderful?

We don't really know anything about this life. We don't really know if our own ideas or the ideas of others are true. We pretend to be experts about the traits of other people but, really, we hardly know ourselves. We don't know who we are.

Isn't it wonderful?

The mind leads us through life with such vivid scenarios and deep programming. We protect ourselves with strategies that brilliant nuclear scientists could design, ignoring what we know we need to do, not recognizing anger that builds inside us, refusing to admit that we love the people we do, in fact, love. Yet it all happens in our little minds instantaneously, without any conscious input.

Isn't it wonderful?

We can live full days connecting with many—even hundreds!—of people in our busy urban settings. Yet, none of these impressions has any lasting effect on the days afterward. We say, "Let's connect," but we don't really. Instead, we live superficially in preference to being touched and held. And we spend decades perfecting this game.

Isn't it wonderful?

We are so sure about our reasoning and opinions. Our arrogance lets us spend much of life certain that we *know*—we know what's right and what's wrong, we know that our needs are greater than the needs of others, we know that we are in OUR power. Of course, there are those diamonds in the rough—those who do not care to be "right" all the time, those who put others before themselves.

Isn't it wonderful?

Here, you go first. Here, let me have the uncomfortable chair. Here, I'll take the smaller portion. This piece looks better, you should take it. I'll be the good one; let's do what you want to do this time. Let's rehash your problems again, I'd really enjoy that.

Isn't it wonderful?

We don't *have* to live any of these unconsciously. But we *do* have to experience it to decide that we are done with it. This is the lesson and the beauty of the dense, material, physical plane. Matter is dense for a reason. It is matched and supported by the science of matter in every way. This is not a coincidence.

I remember trying to give life lessons to my kids when they were young, attempting to save them some grief. But they couldn't follow the advice, just like I couldn't either at their age. My kids were and are great. This is simply our human nature. We aren't ready until we are ready.

Isn't it wonderful?

Once we are ready, we learn life's lessons the good ol' fashioned hard way. We can only reprogram our minds when we dedicate ourselves to the energy of *I'm not going to live that way anymore*—to the realization of our hopes and prayers.

When we love life itself at such an octave that nothing will stand in the way of full-hearted conscious needs and desires (which will drop away), then oh lordy, it's a beautiful day.

Isn't it wonderful?

"The sufferings and problems that you may witness in the life of a person who is trying to become a true disciple or devotee are actually speeding up his or her process of purification." —Amma

Significance: Pluto, critical thinking, weighing options, clarity, transformation, balancing opposites, releasing the unconscious, strength, liberation, purification, stagnation, fear of change

Lessons: The Statesman Elder puts things into perspective and overcomes indoctrination, gaining insight into how we view what happens around us. The Statesman shares how to live in duality and find a working balance based on attuning to the higher "states," beyond an imaginary door. Learn to let situations play out in your life. Judgment is a vanity of the ego. Perception from the ego is always partial and arbitrary.

Practices: Why aren't we listening to our own heart's call? What stands in the way? How can we live as if $2 + 2 = 5$? Reflect on the joy you felt while in your deepest sense of appreciation.

Next Step: Start to live your life in shades of gray, not just in black and white.

Contemplate: There are big and small miracles in our life every day.

Higher Octave: Things happen for me, not to me.

Affirmation: I can learn to see the grace in my life.

19 - THE SUN

For many decades, Michael Jackson kept audiences, fellow artists, the industry around him, and the world on their toes through the magic of his electrifying performances. These performances inspired some to be as talented as he was on the stage. But they can also inspire all of us to express mastery— to endlessly keep honing our craft—on the "stages" available to us, wherever we are.

Experience: Mastery

The 1983 25th anniversary of Motown TV included a historic classic performance of "Billie Jean". That performance was the first time Michael Jackson wore his trademark glove, and the first time he performed the moonwalk dance. Michael carefully planned that performance for maximum impact. In rehearsal he didn't reveal the moonwalk, so *everyone* was surprised by it.

Of course, the song was a smash hit and his dance moves in the video were superlative. I've watched it many times, mesmerized by Jackson's innovation and expression.

The day after that performance. Michael got a call from his idol, Fred Astaire—the first time Fred had called Michael. Fred is quoted as telling Michael, "You're a hell of a mover, man, and you put them on their asses last night." Michael wrote about that call, "It was the greatest compliment I had ever received in my life, and the only one I wanted to believe. For Fred Astaire to say that meant more than anything."

People who are exceptional at what they do set themselves apart. Witnessing someone's mastery of a skill touches us in special ways. When we see human expression at its highest level, it is a transcendental experience for all.

Beethoven, Gauguin, and Ansel Adams are examples of this effect. Frank Lloyd Wright, Michael Jordan, and Meryl Streep will stand out in any age. We appreciate the work of the best chefs, knitters, and quilters. Have you seen Usain Bolt run? Wow! The greatest pole vaulters and shot putters are like dancers. Gardens created by master gardeners and Rose Bowl Parade floats transport us to timeless places. Who doesn't like watching the Olympics, even if it's filled with hours of sports we don't normally follow? When it contains the world's best athletes, somehow it all becomes captivating.

What these talented people have in common is, of course, their mastery of a skill—skills that seem to have taken many lifetimes to build. Each master has their own frequency of expression and, without any trace of ego, they embody their own flavor, robust and full-bodied.

We all possess a unique frequency; otherwise, we would all be the same. Each person differs in our likes and dislikes, talents, and methods of learning and expression. Our unparalleled flavor is an expression of the Divinity unique to each of us. When we can express our flavor freely, others take notice. It does not matter what these masters are doing or how it is expressed. They possess an irresistible gravity.

How about us ordinary people? Well, here is the good news: We are equal to this. We can express, in any moment, a level of mastery over that moment. Elegance and simple grace are available to us in any act we do. Sometimes the difference resides in being free to express our talent without being held back by a lack of success. We become open when we persevere. We relax into what is natural.

The ability to express our own flavor and to live in mastery are examples of living at our highest potential. I see indications of this every day in India, when the accomplishment of even the simplest task can seem extraordinary. The waiter who brings you hot and attractive food is a cause for celebration. The man who cleans your room to a sparkling level is worthy of an extra tip. Even the beggars show off their disfigurations with a sense of pride at having the worst ailment you have ever seen, thus demonstrating how worthy they are of our support.

I have beggar friends who sit every day in the same location, holding their cups for coins with beatific smiles on their faces. In those moments, they are Olympic champions too. India, in a sense, brings us to our knees and teaches us to appreciate the most basic of actions. But shouldn't we all live that way all the time?

There is nothing truly preventing us from living with a sense of mastery. Our abilities are Divine gifts, so it obviously pleases the Gods when we live our highest potential. Be a master of the moment, live with grace and flair, let go of arrogance and the need to control, and the world will smile at the birth of a superstar. Live the intentions you intuit, overcome obstacles one by one, give precious respect to all, and you will see that you too express mastery.

Significance: Sun, self-expression, evolution, creativity, lack of direction, clouds, nourishment, light, sensitivity, reflections, rebirth, transformation, low self-esteem, insecurity, no light

Lessons: The Sun provides all the light, heat, and life in the solar system. We can use that example of concentrated energy as an approach to one-pointedness. Be your best in the moment, moment to moment.

Practices: What unique skills do you possess? What subtle moments have you admired with others in your life? Appreciate what you are and what you have.

Next Step: Show the world your "dance" moves.

Contemplate: Learn your craft each step of the way.

Higher Octave: Appreciate the support you are always receiving.

Affirmation: I am safe, protected, trusting, open, and free.

25

18 – THE MOON

When walking along a dark path in a scary forest, it is easy to feel lost and confused. But within the doubt, Truth is waiting for us to find it. Truth will guide us, just like the Moon is there to guide our way.

Experience: The Devotee's Plea/Dilemma

I can't find my way home,
I go my own way.
What I think is secure is an obstacle,
Using my willpower just blocks the way.
If I am separate, then Divinity is safe,
I can only connect from a place of separation.
I'm afraid to discover that I am God,
But in the desert I can remember my name.
I don't want to dissolve,
I am not protected when I let go.
I'm afraid to become nothing,
Who knows where the time goes?
I can't find my way home.

I wrote these words above— a poem, if you will—one or two years after most of this book was written. More than three years after that, I'm writing this, which is one of the very last themes written for the book. Sometimes we need time to understand the whole story.

I was in Thailand the winter Covid-19 began, and I was reading headlines about a disease in China. For a while, it wasn't much of a story as the numbers were very low. Still, it caught my attention. My departure flight wasn't for quite a few weeks, so I started tracking the cases.

As the world numbers rose, I began having doubts about staying. I decided to visit my airline's local office to see about changing the date of my ticket to an earlier date.

It was quite a walk, so I went early in the day to beat the midday heat. I got there and explained the situation. After some discussion, the airline agent told me I would have to pay a change fee of $100 to leave sooner. Covid wasn't raging and ticket change fees were not yet waived. Instinctively, I rebelled at paying more and impulsively left the office for the long walk home.

I thought later about going back, paying the fee, and changing the ticket, but I never returned to the office. I then considered going to the beach for some weeks before leaving, but I ended up staying put for the remainder of my time. While there was growing concern worldwide, Thailand seemed isolated enough to be safe. I ended up leaving on the flight I had picked more than six months earlier. My return flights were uneventful and safe, but within twenty-four hours of arriving at my U.S. home, the Thailand city and the airport I had flown from AND the U.S. city and airport that I had flown to were "closed." I felt a lot of gratitude for my protection in that situation.

The underlying story started with the long walk home from the airline office. It was late morning/early afternoon by then, and even while walking on the shady side of the street, as I had learned to do there, it was hot. I was a little tired from retracing the route, so, I decided to listen to some music on my phone, which was not something I did very often. It made the walk home feel quicker and more enjoyable, adding a spring to my step.

Something about this day made me jot down some of the songs' lyrics (which you may have noticed). When I got home, I played with the lyrics by adding some "release sentences," resulting in this poem. All lines seem to be non-sequiturs, yet they say the same thing.

When I posted this poem on Facebook, I called it a plea/dilemma. I was still in doubt about leaving. I didn't totally understand it at the time, but those were the words that came. The plea/dilemma is a deep soul call—a climactic moment probably reaching across lifetimes. I couldn't articulate what the plea/dilemma was, but it felt like a primal call for Mother. We need Mother. Mothers radiate a sweet intense energy like no other.

Now, three years later, I can see there was some irony involved that I don't remember seeing then. There I was, trying to get home, writing about how "I can't find my way home" (thank you, Steve Winwood). At the time, the home I couldn't find was spiritual, not a place my airline ticket could take me to. The joke was on me. Thank you, Divinity.

I spent that entire stay in Thailand working on developing intuition and an attitude of surrender, letting go of all positions and positionalities. At that point, I wasn't feeling connected to my intuition, and I felt noticeably unclear about what to do.

I was working with a spiritual practice oriented around removing spiritual blockage and growing intuition. Central to this practice is the use of "release sentences," which help release resistances.

Release sentences are different from affirmations. A given sentence may or may not be true; it doesn't matter. The purpose of saying a release sentence is to identify where the energy of that idea is held in the body. By repeating the phase, you release that energy.

These stuck ideas, captured in the release sentence, can be called "positionalities." They are barriers to being in the state of Peace, Joy, Truth, Bliss and Love. Over years, with ceaseless surrender, this practice became like a mother's love, constant and nourishing.

I see now how much my intuition has grown as a result. The pains have been released. I can see now why this poem is part of the book and why it took three years to manifest. At the time, I pleaded with Spirit to take me home. The cosmic humor of the spiritual quest is that Spirit is screaming at us, in Spirit's own way, that we are already home. Our role is just to realize it. Once we stop looking, we have a better chance of finding what and where home is.

Humans can be a silly lot.

For me, the plea was the heart's longing for clarity. For others, it can feel like unworthiness or thinking our family will not understand us. The dilemma takes the shape of pushing away the very solution we seek. The plea/dilemma is in constant back-and-forth motion between the two extremes, acting as one (not two) energy, until we make peace with both by releasing everything.

"I can't find my way home" contains an implied plea to be shown the way home. By repeating "I can't find my way home" as a release sentence, the pleading energy from the line can be found and released. The plea and dilemma in the poem aren't a plea or dilemma, it is the release of the plea/dilemma energy.

I've found in life that solutions are waiting for problems. When we follow our intuition—our heart, the inner knowing, the inner God—we find our way home. We realize we are always there, even when we don't know it. In the case of my Thailand trip, the ego/mind wanted to move (out of the discomfort of not knowing), but the soul didn't feel a need to move. And the soul won out. In the end, no move was the "right" move. I passed the test without knowing it. And yet, it wasn't a test at all. The idea of "test" was only in my mind. Instead, it was simply an opportunity to learn to release. Three years later, I can see this perspective and have released the devotee's plea/dilemma.

Significance: Pisces, intuition, mother, feminine, finding our way, trusting, nourishment, making actions conscious, wrong turns, surrendering, releasing, deepening consciousness

Lessons: We spend our whole life learning to feel and trust our intuition. The Moon encourages us to be open to going deeper in each opportunity—to live from the heart. We don't ever know the "why", so doing the best we can is the answer to everything.

Practices: Recall a difficult time in your life when the way forward was unclear. Examine how things turned out. Did you have a plea/dilemma? Looking back, can you feel a level of separation from and/or connection to your intuition? If it was both, can you identify what was going on? This is a great opportunity to journal.

Next Step: Do this exercise to feel your intuition speaking to you through any mundane task. Sit and feel what to eat for dinner and where. Sit and wait until you know. Don't "figure" it out with the mind.

Contemplate: Meditate each day and notice the quality of the experience.

Higher Octave: We are always being guided. We aren't always aware of it.

Affirmation: I open my heart for me to see me.

17 – THE STAR

The practice of spiritual sadhana aims to attain a high level of inward Divine connection in the practitioner. New to the practice, we can consider the outer world as a distinct distraction.

Experience: Inward is Never the Wrong Direction

I was fortunate in this life to be able to travel for twenty years, spending winters in Asia and significant time in India each year. I sat meditating in many of India's great saints' bedrooms and meditation spaces. I saw much of the great architecture and have visited sacred pilgrimage spots all over the land, including the great gathering of the Kumbh Mela.

But the heart and soul of India for me became a small nondescript ashram along the banks of the holy Ganga River in the foothills of northern India, where the river first comes out of the mountains. Here, where this ashram sits, the river starts winding 1,560 miles across northern India, from the Himalaya mountains to the Indian Ocean. The Ganges River is not a sacred place; it is a sacred entity.

Known as Ganga Ma—Mother Ganges—the river is revered as a goddess whose purity cleanses the sins of the faithful and aids the dead on their path toward heaven. According to Hindu mythology, the Ganges was once a heavenly river flowing across the sky. Long ago, she agreed to fall to Earth. To prevent the Earth from shattering upon impact, Lord Shiva himself caught Ganges in his hair as she cascaded down from heaven to the Himalayas. Ganges then flowed out of the mountains, across the Indian plains through the heart of India, to the sea.

This ashram was Maharajji's—a humble enlightened master who left his body in his late eighties, towards the end of my twenty-year period of annual travels to Asia.

When he was a young adult, Maharajji went to see his guru to help him with digestive stomach issues. Kneeling to touch his guru's feet, he woke up in that very moment to his True Nature, and his life was changed forever.

Years after this awakening, he graced his ashram, where many Indian disciples lived and where he was everything to his students. He served them all day with prayers and blessings, as teacher, counselor, banker, and general life adviser. Maharajji was like the head of a giant family in this traditional conservative Indian ashram. His stomach issues were never healed.

He was part of a very powerful lineage of a few great gurus who are not particularly known by history. Among the few stories told of these great souls, I remember one in which a guru dropped his old-aged body by waking up a young, dead body lying along the Ganga. He touched the body's third eye, then walked away in the new body, which he had brought back to life.

One sensed the sacred shakti (powerful energy) that had been passed from master to master in this lineage.

Sitting with a guru (which means "giver of light" in Hindi) is an ancient tradition in India.

This is how teachers transmit transformational teachings that help students transcend to higher vibrations in the light. The teachers are there to light our way on the path.

While we look to the teacher for their light, the teacher is constantly trying to ignite the light in us. The teacher points to the light of the star within us, not in themselves. This is the same flow from the beginning of time. Light emanates from the stars and then from the heavenly river to the earthly sacred river, then to the teacher, and finally to the student. This flow of light is the answer to our soul's call for hope and prayer. All we need is here.

But this resource is disappearing in India as the wise old teachers leave their bodies. There are fewer of them to shine light on the path. Life in India has changed like everywhere else in the world, with overpopulation and the disappearance of unspoiled areas. The pace of modern life is replacing peace.

In the mid-1980s, a young Western woman walked into the ashram and became Maharajji's disciple. By the time I walked into the ashram, ShantiMayi was a guru herself and was gathering with more than a hundred Westerners each winter. Things had changed in this traditional Indian ashram. It was a real meeting of East and West—very unusual for traditional India. Satsangs—heart-opening community sessions during which we all shared issues of the heart—occurred daily. I have many beautiful memories of those days when the light I am passing to you was passed to me.

The winters I spent in India featured an array of amazing musicians and we sang together in bliss, sometimes for an hour a day. I want to share one of these powerful sacred chants with you here. It suggests how to light that star within.

Inward is never the wrong direction,
outward is always an inner reflection.
I know that I am, but I do not know why.
What peace this wisdom brings.

The quiet that comes from inward reflection can give us new understanding of our outer life. Everything is connected. Like a wish upon a star, this practice can light our way and answer our prayers. In these four lines I see a universal wish, hope, prayer, and an answer. Peace is the hope and the answer to our prayers. All life is a teacher when we see it that way.

Significance: Aquarius, hope, growth, renewal, peace, light, confusion, optimism, freedom, spiritual growth, challenges, talents, stagnation, imprisonment, greener pastures, great mother

Lessons: The Star—who we really are—is always with us, whether we see it or not. There is a plan influencing our every move. Life always allows us to tap into this wisdom in the quiet inner world.

Practices: Make some time in your day for inward reflection. Can you see how your thinking affects your outward reality? Have you experienced light coming to or from you?

Next Step: Sit quietly for some time each day and feel joy within yourself.

Contemplate: Each moment, I am loved by the Universe.

Higher Octave: I can tap into the light whenever I want.

Affirmation: My path is always illuminated, whether I know it or not.

16 – THE TOWER

Birds' migrations can be used as a symbol to remind us that everything changes. All birds need to find a good place to feed and breed. But those places change with the seasons. A perfect summer home can become uninhabitable in winter. A hero's journey and a true rite of passage, birds fly thousands of miles through arduous and changing conditions to reach the right place for the right season of their life.

Experience: Impermanence

Impermanence is a big word that has a depth that not everyone may be familiar with. This concept is essential to both Buddhism and Hinduism. It simply means that everything changes all the time. Nothing in life is permanent.

Many people, by nature, are adversely affected by change. They want life to stay the same, so they fight change by resisting it. Simple adjustments in daily routines or larger modifications like vacations, moves, and death can create a sense of imbalance.

Fighting change is an attempt to exert our will over our circumstances. Some people deny change, then get angry or depressed at their lack of control. At some point, a measure of acceptance may appear. Until we learn to flow with impermanence and see the good that change provides, it can knock us around.

Human nature has difficulty living in the moment. Our minds are always seeking the future. This applies to every aspect of life.

Let's take for example, being in a new relationship. At the initial stage there is a natural enthusiasm and excitement. And yet, we start looking ahead. We want to know what the future of the relationship holds and when we will feel settled.

The second stage is the fixed stage. This is perhaps the longest and most stable stage, when things become mundane. Fault-finding and dull routines start developing. During this time, we may begin to desire "fresh" aspects to the relationship.

The third stage is mutable, during which there are aspects of the first two stages at play. We look forward to getting back to the newness and excitement of the first stage, but we also look forward to the comfort of the second stage.

We don't know what will happen in the relationship; each day is different and unpredictable. Friends ask, "Are you still together?" We say, "Depends on the day." The mutable stage is characterized by changes and moment-to-moment uncertainty.

This wheel of life is very hard to get off.

When we are present and at ease with our current stage, we can find peace and stop longing for the next one, as if it were a greener pasture. In relationships, just like life, change is inevitable. The key is to enjoy the current moment, whatever it is, rather than resisting it in favor of some future vision.

It's the same for a job: We start with enthusiasm and hope, then feel boxed in. Eventually, we wonder if we will quit or be fired first. Child rearing, gaining in-laws, and owning a house or a car can all undergo these same stages.

I respect change. Change is a persistent part of life. To overcome the difficulties of change, we must learn to accept things as they are. I've worked to become totally present to and appreciative of my current stage of life. I know things will change, so I've stopped looking ahead.

By being in the present, I'm more able to respect and accept the change when it comes. I am more open and vulnerable to it. I am in each NOW, knowing the now will change. That is the practice.

While we know change will affect the parts of life we like, it will also change the things we struggle with. This too will change. Let that be our mantra.

One part of impermanence that I like the best is that because everything changes naturally, I don't have to feel responsible for everything in my life that needs change.

Do I still work on bettering myself? Yes, but I can relax without a sense of rigidity, burden, or rightness around my challenges. I can appreciate that I am doing the best that I can. Do I still need to work on getting a new job or new house? Yes, I need to work on providing for my wants and needs. But I can release any feeling of responsibility that if I don't do it, nothing will happen. Change happens in its own time. The right job or house will come along. I still need to do my part, but I don't have to feel burdened by my role or the uncertainty of the outcome.

Let's work together to see impermanence as our friend. Change is the nature of evolution. We don't often immediately see the benefits of change, but over the long term, the truth becomes clear. Like the migration of birds with the changing of seasons or the final unfolding of the butterfly after breaking free from its chrysalis, we can see life through the lens of accepting what comes our way as a gift.

Significance: Mars, change, overcoming difficulties, releasing old beliefs, new insights, self-awareness, destruction, revolution, fiery feelings, dependency, freedom, oneness

Lessons: The Tower teaches us that one thing we can count on is change. While we may not like a particular change, the power of impermanence is central to the flow of life. Working with it, not against it, opens us to beauty.

Practices: Honestly, how are you doing with change in your life? Do you live thinking about greener pastures? How can you be more present in the "now" of your life?

Next Step: Breathe deeply with any changes that are hard for you.

Contemplate: Everything changes.

Higher Octave: Appreciate the freedom impermanence creates.

Affirmation: I can see the good that comes from every change in my life.

15 – THE DEVIL

We deflect a lot of energy that comes to us because feeling it can be painful. But in deflecting, we lose the opportunity to feel pain, release it, and be free of suffering.
Getting sidetracked by deflecting discomfort will keep us from pursuing the true road ahead.

Experience: The Deflection Agenda

I once had a young client who demonstrated an extreme case of avoidance. In the initial part of our work together, she ignored, denied, and countered whatever I said. It was her attempt to shield herself from things that, deep down, she knew were true. Because of her inability to identify her actions, I named this behavior "The Deflection Agenda.".

This client was looking like a third base coach in baseball, sending hand signals to the batter. She was folding her arms, touching her nose, and pointing while she blamed, contradicted, and ignored.

Deflection is a defense mechanism described in psychology as a way people distance themselves from a full awareness of unpleasant thoughts, feelings, and behaviors. It is avoiding or turning aside.

These actions are unconscious. If confronted, we often deny the deflection. It is natural to deny the reality of our uncomfortable behaviors because they are mostly invisible to us, making them difficult to acknowledge.

We like to think that we are defending "the self" —what we think is the highest version of our self—when we deflect. However, we are really defending the ego—the personality or self that the mind creates. It's sticky and invisible.

There are plenty of approaches for wielding deflection: Anger, fear, and shame; blaming others; over-rationalizing; overthinking; out-talking and changing the subject; becoming defensive. It's all an attempt to keep ourselves safe. It's like we are on a dance floor using our moves to hide and side-step.

But does this work? Not in the long term. I know this from my own behavior, which my wife has pointed out on a few occasions. Sometimes when we discuss serious subjects like death, I make inappropriate jokes and try to change the subject. I do this because of my own discomfort with the subjects. Thankfully, the reminder helps me cultivate awareness in those moments.

The deflection agenda drops when we start to relax and face what is being revealed. We can change our attitude in twenty to thirty minutes, sometimes after tears and heartfelt emotions. When we become aware of our actions, we can understand how we hurt ourselves or others. We hurt ourselves when we don't allow ourselves to feel the hard feelings; when we don't act from integrity. We hurt others when our deflective behavior turns outward and becomes accusatory. When we deflect, we are not very aware. We get stubborn, self-absorbed, and closed-minded.

Growth in life depends on our ability to observe our own behavior. Letting go of arrogances — "I know better, I can't be wrong, I am right, I am indestructible" — is important.

It helps to breathe deeply. It helps to relax. It is necessary to be open to new ideas, to let love and appreciation shine through. Because the deflection agenda is instinctive and difficult to see in ourselves, accepting support from those we trust can help.

Like my wife, others can call our attention to our deflection agenda. In recognizing it, we can chip away at it little by little. This kind of behavior may be hardened by decades of unexamined habit. But like the rocks tumbled by the river, it will become smooth over time. Being honest with ourselves will help, as will asking for others' feedback.

Becoming aware of our feelings, then releasing the energy behind the feelings, is the path to peace. We can live free by owning up to our deflection agenda.

Significance: Capricorn, defending, insecurity, discipline, straight line, compulsions, obsessions, negative habits, illusion, fear, worry, concern, overcoming personal fears

Lessons: Residual anger, resentments, and conditioning from childhood can solidify into personality strategies. This Devil in us reflects to us how we appear to others. It can take a lifetime to minimize these strategies.

Practices: How do you protect yourself by deflecting? How much? Be honest. What might life be like if you were able to reduce these behaviors?

Next Step: Learn to observe your own actions and behaviors objectively.

Contemplate: How sticky and obnoxious your behavior can be.

Higher Octave: Take in what people say, good and bad. Instead of becoming defensive, use it as an opportunity to grow.

Affirmation: I can master all situations that appear in my life.

14 – THE PEACEMAKER

I consider the concept of time to be ancient humanity's first concept. This wisdom was based on their observation of the day-to-night sky and the changes in seasons. Then, in a moment of arrogance, the thought came that we, humanity, could master nature. This, I consider the ancients' second concept: humanity is more powerful and intelligent than nature. With this thought came a need to control life. When we release our arrogant conviction that we are and know better, we can find peace within.

Experience: Arrogance

A long time ago, when I was in my mid-twenties, before my children were born, I lived in Oregon on a big piece of forested land. It was the Christmas season, and my wife went home to the Midwest to see her family while I stayed alone in a ten-foot by ten-foot, uninsulated cabin that we had built.

The cabin had no electricity, but it did have kerosene lamps and a wood stove. It might be hard to imagine living this way now, but at the time (the early 1970s), we found it valuable.

Possibly as a test of wills, we were inspired by Thoreau's *Walden* experience of living off the land as a method of self-discovery. I could spin many stories from this time of my life, but I want to share one aspect of my secluded holiday season.

I worked outside all day, but at night I sat in the lone chair in the cabin and read by the light of a kerosene lamp. I wore everything I could because it was cold. I lived in a forest and had plenty of firewood, but for some reason, I didn't often make fires during those couple of weeks that I lived alone.

Looking back at this period, I'd say it was arrogance on my part to be sitting in the cold. I thought I was above being cold, that I was better than needing a fire. This kind of arrogance is an attitude that can leave us very cold and alone.

According to a dictionary definition, arrogance is "an overbearing pride evidenced by a superior manner toward inferiors." I see it in clients and friends, I see it in people on the streets, and I see it in myself. It is an *I know better, I am better, you can't touch me* attitude. This superior manner shows up as deflection, anger, judgment, defensiveness, running away, rudeness, and lots of other low vibration ways of being.

I'm not judging this behavior; we have all acted this way at one time or another. But it gets in the way of our growth and inhibits our ability to hear others around us. Arrogance—that egoic pride that we are better and superior—keeps us separate from others and from the natural world. As we feel less than others—less than what we think we "should" be—we compensate with a superficial superior stance that fools nobody.

Arrogance is a powerful two-edged sword in our human life. On one hand, we need reassurance that we can safely transcend (or at least accept) our natural human vulnerability and insecurities. But at some point, we need to learn not to cut with the sword—to grow beyond our defiant stances and soften into a natural security about our own authority and competence.

How can we let go of arrogance?

Well, it isn't the first thing that drops off as we start on the path of self-growth, that's for sure. To break free from arrogance, most of us need to develop other skills first. The ability to observe our own actions dispassionately is a good first step. Then, the ability to be authentic and honest with ourselves about our actions and behaviors will help. Developing a softness by opening our heart and feeling compassion toward self and others is necessary too.

Having a supportive group around you can help you as you release your need to exhibit this behavior. I would say arrogance begets arrogance, just as it's challenging to stop smoking if you are hanging with a bunch of smokers. It helps to have a close, caring companion—someone understanding and supportive who can build you up (like and love you) when you act in high-handed ways. Supportive, skillful others can be mirrors who enable us to see ourselves the way others see us.

As we become more secure and confident, arrogance is no longer a main force in our life. It will only appear at times of insecurity. After the thirties, arrogance naturally subsides as our need to justify ego-driven ways of being decreases. However, arrogance can still create hindrances to our living in presence in more subtle ways, like keeping our heart closed to others. Eventually we can learn to trust *self*, not ego.

When we're all one, there is no superior or inferior. We see this in the humility of the elderly. We all feel them, and they touch our heart. But we don't have to be elderly to live this simplicity. We just need to drop our armor relating to others. I want to encourage all of you to be on the lookout for arrogance. It can be insidious, like the darkness that hides danger and mystery on a path. Don't judge it, don't judge yourself, just light a lamp of wisdom to see that your highest good is not served by arrogance.

Significance: Sagittarius, expansion, testing wills, fiery tests, inner change, internal fire, high values, cleansing, balance, finding equilibrium, patience, moderation, practice grace

Lessons: To be the Peacemaker, we must learn control of our inner fires. Subtle jabs of superiority have become very commonplace in modern society. The one who sees the self clearly finds life to be a level playing field, all things as they are.

Practices: In what ways might you be arrogant? How have others behaved arrogantly with you? How would life be if you felt balanced all the time?

Next Step: What would happen if we dropped all the armor and swords that we brandish to defend ourselves?

Contemplate: We don't have to be arrogant; it's an old habit that we can reduce over time until it loses its power over us.

Higher Octave: Being kind, forgiving, and compassionate will assist our pursuit of spiritual goals.

Affirmation: I love myself as I am.

13 – DEATH

*Flying high above the clouds with Earth invisible below,
we feel closer to heaven and our heavenly self. We have no control
over the plane. There is nothing to do but "be".
Enjoy these moments of practice: trusting and accepting what is.*

Experience: I Die Daily

A reality we all share is that, at some point, the body will die. I've read that at our birth, the time of death is set but not the method. How we get there and how we feel about it is very individual. It is something we can feel a need to be prepared for.

We prepare for death by living. By living consciously, we experience each moment fully. Then, death becomes just another moment.

For many years, I have experienced leaving my USA life for a season of travel abroad. That plane trip, usually twenty-four hours or more, is like a little death. I can't go anywhere. I have one reality: eating, reading, resting/sleeping, thinking, and movies. Sitting and waiting is the overriding energy. I have learned to love this transition time. After days or weeks of preparation, I have the chance to just be—be in the plane with absolutely no control. I love it. No agenda, no choice, just time to be.

How do we practice this when we're not on an airplane?

I suggest sitting in the family room with loved ones around us. Go quiet and don't move. For a time, allow life and kids to go on around us but say and do nothing. Practice squinting the eyes and seeing/not seeing. How does this feel?

At work, sit back in your chair and go limp for a minute or two. Listen to the noise of your workplace without any involvement in it. Have no opinions or needs. Forget what needs to be done or what was just done. Be like a light fixture hanging on the ceiling or a mop resting in the corner.

In the supermarket, stop for a minute. Feel the energy and desires of the shoppers. Practice feeling the kids wanting stuff, and step back from being there at the same time. Have no agenda, no needs, no opinions. Then, return to animation and feel it more completely.

Sit on a park bench and disappear the same way. The more crowded the park, the better. Stop moving, close your eyes, listen, then even stop listening. Disappear into a void that has no agenda or momentum. Be free to just "be" for as long as you can.

This is like sleep, but it is not sleep. It is a means of practicing for the big sleep by learning non-attachment to your life. I am suggesting we do this in a way that feels more conscious, not less conscious. It isn't small but large. We become quiet but not unaware.

I was in New York a few months ago and sat in the park where I used to play more than sixty years prior. How wonderful it was to just be, talking to no one, knowing and somehow not knowing. I noticed many changes to that place while being invisible and visible at the same time.

Imagine the feeling that all our "to do" lists are extraneous. Imagine no more cooking, eating, and bathing—no more places to drive to and no more sunsets. How does that feel? Whatever comes up, look at it deeply.

I had a teacher say we have died and reincarnated thousands of times. It was said in a very matter-of-fact way. The way she said that, years ago, made me relax about death in ways I had not done before. It will be an old friend when I get there. How nice it is to meet an old friend again! It is one of the best feelings.

To be ready, though, it seems we need to do the work each day. We are gifted the opportunity each day with sleep, ending one day and beginning the next hours later. We close our eyes and, one by one, each sense stops and disappears. When we relax, we drift off to sleep. It's not a big deal. In that drift, there are no thoughts of things undone or concerns of the next day. We're just adrift in an aimless motion, carried on unseen currents. We don't fight this; it feels rather natural. It pulls us, and we are okay with it.

This is the daily preparation. It happens when we tell our loved ones how we feel each day. It happens when we are completely at work and the market. It happens when we take time to sit in the park. Sit on a park bench and watch a sunset so you will be prepared. Know that we are guided by an unseen-yet-familiar shepherd each and every moment. If this guide is not an angel, it is at least an inner knowing that we can explore and use as a compass. No time and effort in these pursuits is wasted. Be in the life, then be able to let it go. Practice I die daily.

Significance: Scorpio, death, transformation, sadness, vulnerability, control, endings, rebirth, creativity, evolution, catalyst, impediments, no alignment, frustration, fear

Lessons: Death is a natural process that is sacred and holy. So is all change that comes into our life. We can work on non-attachment every day.

Practices: Explore how you feel when your life goes quiet, like on an airplane when there is nothing you can or are able to do… Are there aspects of your death that you have been avoiding? Do you think there is a soul that is immortal?

Next Step: Practice being conscious while falling asleep.

Contemplate: How good it feels to release burdens and failures.

Higher Octave: Being at peace with the flows of life.

Affirmation: Every experience of life offers wisdom.

12 – THE HANGED MAN

A cow and a fence are a combination we see everywhere in the world.
We drive by them mindlessly.
But they can be the makings of a marvelous teaching.

Experience: Untie the Rope

At times, we can feel really stuck in our mental stories, unable to see beyond the illusionary nature of our mind. We get so tangled in our made-up beliefs that we can't escape the concrete mental bunker box they create.

We imagine only the best furnishings in this prison. We believe our self-created jail cells are "livable" if they have the biggest TVs or the best sound systems, or the perfect kitchen appliances. Lovely decorations can justify staying locked up in our cell. We get invested in the opinion that living with what we already know is best, even if it is painful and brings suffering. It certainly must be better than recklessly dropping the story and stepping into an unknown freedom.

We tell ourselves that when we meet someone, life will be perfect. We hold onto the idea that a promotion at work is all we want in life. We think that once we move, our life will settle down.

For some, the prospect of freedom strips us of our defenses, leaving us naked and vulnerable. It seems dangerous, even crazy, to release the identities and personalities we take for granted.

I've danced with people in different ways to try to put cracks in those prison walls. For some, even if I find a door and throw it open wide for them, still, it is very hard to leave their cell. Like a caged bird who won't fly out of an open door, the mind can argue convincingly that the unpleasant known is better than unknown possibilities.

What to do? I've had success with the following teaching story from India. The simple universality of stories like this is part of why they are so endearing.

A cow herder wanted to tie up his cow for the evening, but he didn't have a rope. So, he decided to go to his Guru to ask for advice. He went to the Guru and told him of his predicament. The Guru said, "Tie him up with an imaginary rope." So, the cow herder went home and tied his cow up with an imaginary rope. He slept very well that night.

In the morning, he wanted to walk the cow to his field, but the cow wouldn't move. He sat for some time trying to figure out what to do. Eventually, he went back to his Guru and told him of his predicament. The Guru said, "You need to untie the imaginary rope." The cow herder went home, untied the imaginary rope, and walked the cow to his field.

A spiritual life unties imaginary ropes. We are not our stories. They help us to navigate life but, in identifying with these stories, we live as a personality, tying ourselves down with imaginary ropes of limited possibilities.

Our work is to untie the ropes and exit through open doors. With practice, we learn to recognize when we hold ourselves back with imaginary stories. Some people are really blessed because they can HEAR the mental stories and do the work of coming back to the moment without getting stuck in judgments. For others, it takes effort to come back to the moment. With practice, we learn to never leave.

One can quickly feel positive effects of untying. The heart relaxes and we breathe deeper. The lasting effects take a bit longer but are oh-so rewarding.

The ultimate trick is to remember that there's nothing to "do," other than remain calm while simultaneously recognizing the dynamic nature of our expanded sense of freedom. Be still there. Learn to recognize when you start to drift away from that place and bring yourself back each time. Over time, these course corrections come easier. Give the self "permission" to come to and live and be.

The brain will rebel, so give it permission to "stand down" from thinking it knows better. When we do this, tense energy in the body will shift back into the buoyancy that is a natural by-product of living in the stillness. The mind will obey by going quiet when it knows the game is over. There's a new sheriff in town!

Feel the essence of the self without the noisy mental chatter and illusory roadblocks that previously seemed so necessary. Ride the unimpeded flow to the innermost self. This has always been what we can call our purpose. This wise and timely counsel will carry us over the threshold that seemed impassable before.

I have found awakening to be an experience of remembering rather than the creation of a new experience. All that happens is part of the process—we are all One. We can live that way when we untie the rope.

Significance: Neptune, changing perspective, unfolding of life, relaxation, acceptance, getting unstuck, new ways, surrender, holding on to expectations, internal freedom

Lessons: It is easy to become the Hanged Man by blaming outside circumstances or other people for the difficulties we encounter. It is important to realize the power our minds have in determining our beliefs. Untying the imaginary ropes of our life and releasing positions we hold is the path to freedom.

Practices: Examine the prison of your own creation. What would it feel like to open that exit door and step through? What do we actually control in this life?

Next Step: Begin to realize how thoughts limit choices.

Contemplate: Possessions and thoughts can weigh us down.

Higher Octave: Freedom comes from within and is free.

Affirmation: I own nothing, I am free. In myself, I am free.

11 – SPIRITUAL TRUTH

*The magical first steps of a baby are treasured by all parents.
Anything we achieve in life starts with that same magical first step.
To recognize the magic, it helps to be a little innocent and naïve
instead of focusing on a distant, sometimes arbitrary, goal.*

Experience: You Only Need to Know the First Step

For many of my clients, hearing what they need to "do" to be whole and acceptable in their own eyes, initially feels very deflating. It's understandable. We stand at the foot of a huge mountain, thinking, *That is a tall mountain! Can I really climb it?* But the path to the top already exists. So, I tell them, "Just start with the first step. We don't need to know the last step at this point, just the first."

I learn this in my own projects which are born from a simple inspiration, just like a few moments ago, when I began writing this theme. I have no idea how it will end. I don't need to know right now. I just need to write this sentence, and the next one will come. Somehow, at the end, it is done. Step-by-step— that's how our lives move forward (flow), even if we don't see it that way.

The solutions to problems that we don't yet know exist are already waiting for us. Yes, frequently the solution is already in place, waiting for the problem. Car mechanics have studied their trade and opened their shops waiting for us and our automobiles to have a problem. Farmers are growing food today for our meals tomorrow.

Trust that we are guided along our path. Our work is to take one first manageable step. The next step will follow, then many more, taking us closer to our goals.

Significance: Leo, beginnings, first step, truth, courage, action, challenges, morals, growth, strength, acceptance, intensity, fairness

Lessons: Taking a first step toward any spiritual goal is the most important step, until the next. There is only ever one step in front of us. The simplicity of this lesson does not diminish its value as a Spiritual Truth.

Practices: What are your resistances? Does a fear of failure paralyze you? Imagine how good accomplishment feels, then project that on to a difficulty.

Next Step: The next step is the next step, with all the courage of the first step.

Contemplate: Step-by-step, I can accomplish whatever I want.

Higher Octave: The Universe conspires to manifest what the heart calls out for.

Affirmation: I am more powerful than I realize.

10 – FORTUNE

*Sunflowers teach us to keep facing the Sun in life.
The Sun feeds us, keeps us warm, and offers us light.
It provides a path in life and helps us out of moods, brightening our days. Without the Sun, there would be no life in the solar system.
Both the Sun and the sunflower want us to learn our worth.*

Experience: Prosperity Consciousness, a Measure of Self-Worth

Prosperity consciousness is tuning in to that which sustains us and enhances our full blossoming as spiritual beings.

In our ordinary society, prosperity consciousness gets mixed up with money. Money becomes a very loaded word, getting confused with accomplishment, productivity, and self-esteem. But ultimately, money is energy. We do need some money for everyday life to buy things for our survival. But it can become a measure used for our ego's projections and a distraction from more important goals. We can set goals for money; for prosperity, we need to go deeper.

Prosperity is really an inward game. If one wants to prosper, then one needs to love the self and be able to value the self as it is—naked, with our limitations and baggage exposed. Beyond accumulating money, prosperity is progressing to a place in life that feels "right" to us. "Right" means dharmic, conscious, and with integrity—a win-win.

Being conscious is being aware and accepting—being alert with an inner *knowing*. Consciousness is the substance of everything. It's the playing field of all existence. It's like oxygen for breathing, but more expansive to include All. Prosperity consciousness allows *self* to fully flower.

In India, we experience people who are prosperous and have literally nothing. I walk past a man every day—a "holy beggar" in white—who sits and asks for nothing but has peace. Would you say such a man does not have prosperity consciousness?

Significance: Jupiter, expansion, flow, love, openness, challenges, growth, freedom, self-worth, satisfaction, smallness, disharmony, stagnation, honesty

Lessons: We can make our own fortune by being open to what is. It starts with seeing the self as worthwhile. To see our challenges as opportunities is the fortune of the wise. Living this way, moment-to-moment, is our highest potential.

Practices: What are your real goals in life? What do you most admire in other people? What limits you from feeling prosperous?

Next Step: If something is possible, then assume it will happen without having to know when.

Contemplate: How do I sabotage my own expressions?

Higher Octave: Feeling gratitude for life and each moment as it is.

Affirmation: I can create my own fortune and feel fortunate.

9 – THE HERMIT

There is a biblical teaching that says, "Be in the world, but not of it." I first heard this early in my spiritual training, so it's something I've tried to live with for a while. To be "in the world" is to create, explore, inquire, discover, expand, and multiply. To be "of it" is to embrace opinions, judgements, comparisons, expectations, righteous thinking, gossip, self-diminishing thoughts, or their like. It is best to avoid these.

Experience: Emptiness

Emptiness is the same as silence. It is not "no noise." It is "no story." To be empty of story means that you live in stillness, and all movement is from a *higher truth*. There is peace that surrounds emptiness. and this peace contains everything.

When most people hear the word emptiness, they often think of a void—a black hole they will get sucked into and never escape. We fear that in such a place, we would feel alone and lacking. This is interesting because the *real* sticky, sucking black hole is a mind full of thoughts. Emptiness is not about a lack of value, significance, or meaning. Rather, it's about not clinging to or holding on to anything—thoughts, ideas, or possessions.

There is a cultural war going on inside people all over the world. Our modern societies make us think we need more possessions to be happy. To lack possessions means there is something lacking in our lives. Yet, possessions don't fulfill us in the deepest ways. In fact, the pursuit of possessions creates more suffering inside of us. In order to feel whole, we need to do less and be more.

"I am nothing" can also mean that we don't define our self by what we accomplish; that in simply being we feel connected to all life and the natural world; that the song of the morning bird and the wind through the tree brings tears to our eyes; that to see children playing in innocence, without a need or concern in the world other than that moment, takes our breath away; that the poise we see in our friend makes us think of the Mona Lisa.

Nothing *is* everything. It allows an inner silence which has nothing missing. I invite all to turn down the noises of life. Go to your *knowing*. Let go of the voices in the head. Drop fully into each breath. Find everything you seek. Be the emptiness that is already inside you.

Significance: Virgo, communication, solidifying in *self*, appreciation of being alone, being in nature, quiet within, center, authenticity, busy mind, looking for distractions, separation

Lessons: Do not fear missing out. Like the Hermit, being on a solitary path can lead to higher vibrations and clarity in all directions. Silence and quiet offer us an opportunity to listen and learn.

Practices: What are the noises in your life? How are your thoughts unhealthy? Count your blessings.

Next Step: Spend more quiet time outside to gain inside quiet. Gift the self with many opportunities in quiet.

Contemplate: The emptier I am, the more I can live in truth.

Higher Octave: I live in calm during the storms of life.

Affirmation: I relish, in richness, my time alone.

8 – KARMA

*Sometimes it seems stuff happens merely to wake us up.
Things may continue to happen until we cry out for help.
Crying out for help can mean stopping and observing our self with
objectivity. The sooner we learn a lesson, the easier it is.
Lessons will circle back and intensify the more we disregard them.
The wound that isn't treated can become infected.*

Experience: Everything is a Teaching

Yesterday, a short clip of a talk by Jetsunma Tenzin Palmo appeared on my Facebook news feed. Years ago, I was fortunate to be able to spend thirty minutes alone in her presence. She is a long-time Western Buddhist nun and became well known for her book, *Cave in the Snow*, about her twelve years meditating in a cave in northern India. I do recommend that readers check out her book.

In the clip, she talked about an incident from the years she spent in the cave. It was snowing late in the winter season and because the ground had already thawed, there were drops of water dripping everywhere around her.

She already had a cold, so she moved the box that she used for meditation and sleeping in an upright position to minimize the drops landing on her. In this moment, the thought came that perhaps others were right; her commitment to living in the cave was not such a good idea.

We have all experienced doubts, questioning what's happening to us. Some of us blame and shame ourselves, thinking, *What an idiot I am, how stupid can I be, why didn't I listen to....?* Sometimes we blame others and instinctively lash out with criticism. However, this is an ideal time to look past our reactions to see the truth that everything that happens to us is a teaching.

In reviewing her Buddhist teachings, it occurred to Jetsunma that it was perfectly alright for things not to be alright. Circumstances only become hard when we label difficulties as difficult. There are problems or situations that we wish were different, but if we stop labeling them as problems, we see that everything is fine as it is.

Sometimes things go well, other times not as well. Does it really matter? Situations become problematic when they're weighed down by the mind. In accepting life as it is, a huge weight is removed from our backs.

She ended her talk with this wisdom, "It is our resistance that makes the pain, painful. There is no problem in having problems."

When a problem reveals itself, you can practice not labeling it as a problem. I had one of those India stories going on this week. My toilet was not working effectively. I started getting a head cold and a little fever. Then the guesthouse's internet went down. This was a great opportunity to react and feel bummed. What happened next? After a day, the internet started working again. I took it easy, slept, ate soup, and started feeling better. I realized that I could use the shared toilet downstairs until mine was fixed by the busy plumber. Everything is a teaching. My lessons were patience, flexibility, and faith.

People talk about Mercury retrograde as a time when everything breaks and people are confused. I think it is a time to release our constant expectations of others and of life itself. Maybe the Universe is trying to tell us something when we don't get our way. It's our job to listen and learn.

Listening comes when we calm the chatter of the mind. Stuck in the mind, we cannot hear anything. Listening comes by living in the heart. You may ask, "Won't we miss stuff if we don't think it through?" On the contrary. My experience is that I catch more living from the heart. I miss stuff when I am stuck in the mind.

When we can look at our lives and our reactions to life with a bit of perspective, we can see how we are always supported by the cosmic intelligence that provides all we need. The ability to grow food, the food appearing in our stores, our body digesting our food. We can see this is a miracle—even a series of miracles. When we do, we open to the awareness that everything in our life is a teaching.

Significance: Libra, balance, difficulties, growth, acceptance, making problems, the gift of life, strength, perseverance, conscious choice, perceptive, courage, forward action

Lessons: Karma (union with God through action) can be viewed as happening to us, but it can also be for us, helping to zero in on our next lesson. Inspiration can lift us above karma to a higher frequency. Learn to be your own strength and courage.

Practices: Name some things you take for granted. How does life support you? Meditate on how life gave you a little thing, and it will blow your mind.

Next Step: When something "bad" happens to you, be open to considering whether it is actually "bad."

Contemplate: How big do we make our problems? Imagine observing one of your "problems" from outer space, or from one hundred years in the future. How big is this problem from those perspectives?

Higher Octave: Appreciation for our karma that holds, carries, and supports us.

Affirmation: I feel safe in the winds of life.

7 – THE PRODIGY

A beautiful flower is busy. Busy doing nothing. But is it?

*Flowers are built for attraction with fragrance, elegance, and beauty.
They attract birds and insects for pollination. Flowers contain the
reproductive part of the plant and are responsible for its survival.
To us, flowers are seen as symbols of love, peace, and joy.
They provide comfort in times of sorrow, reducing anxiety and stress.
Flowers can also be a source of nutrition and medicinal healing.
Without flowers, there are no grains, nuts, or berries. Flowers teach us
that we don't have to be actively engaged to accomplish in this life.*

Experience: Busy Doing Nothing

There are times in life when we are so proud of our accomplishments. We list them on our social media as if they define us, to let the world know… that we belong? That we are worthy? That we are trustworthy? That we are capable?

The answers as to why we list them are varied depending on the nature of our contact with the world. Of course, our contact changes over the course of our life. Generally, as we get older, we have less need to be seen and heard because we feel seen and heard from within.

When I get together with one of my friends in India, I inquire about how he is doing. His standard answer is, "I am busy. I am busy doing nothing."

Now, you must understand that this man, Swami Atmananda Udasin, is always serving others. There was a time in our friendship when he was sleeping very little. His entire day was filled with visitors whom he counseled and taught, all while running his facility where he is responsible for taking care of and feeding others, staff included. He communicates regularly with many people, often setting up ambitious traveling schedules for himself. Then, late at night when all other duties are put to bed for the day, he works on his own projects, including editing books written by people he admires for publication in different languages. His use of the word "nothing," does not mean NOTHING. But what does he mean?

Knowing my friend, I believe he means that nothing we do in life is all that important. Certainly, it is not important enough to develop egotistical attitudes about. I think he means that, deep within, he is not attached to what he does. This is a man who has long been on the spiritual path, and his nature won't allow using accomplishments to define his self.

Busy doing nothing is a deep teaching. It encourages us to develop humility. It demonstrates that, in reality, what we do is not so important or long-lasting. We are born, we make a mark perhaps, and we disappear. How simple and complete.

We can get a very insulated view, thinking that what we do is important, special, and needed. Our need to feel special comes from our insecurities about our place in life. When we don't feel secure within, we look for validation from others. We seek praise and congratulations.

I like to view this from a perspective of small view to big view. If needing to be important is a small view, what does the big view look like?

The big view asks, What did I come here to do? Why are we here?

But there is nothing to do. My friend is telling us that.

Life is more about being and experiencing than working through a giant to-do list. I've come to see life as an expression of creative forces that are there to be lived. Life is not about doing; it is about being.

The cosmic intelligence is not about control, but it does have a flow. What are the expressions of life? What are the board game pieces we use? Try these on: vibration, energy, frequency, chi, numbers, color, sound, wind, sunshine, gravity, catalysts—yum. The artist's palette has colors and brushes. The musician has notes, melody, and rests. We humans have them all. It doesn't matter what we accomplish or do. We honor the flow by using the tools; it is not about the products we create with them.

Imagine God saying to you, "My job is to take you beyond your mind. How can I take you beyond your mind when you are stuck in your mind? Often, I do not answer in the way you want me to. Those who know me are very used to that."

Be with these words for a few moments. And then be again with what my dear wise friend says, "I am busy. I am busy doing nothing."

Significance: Cancer, arrogance, emotional breakthrough, introspection, adolescent energy, coming of age, pride, ego's drive, flow, full flowering, finding balance in action

Lessons: We all have inherent skills and are The Prodigy in one way or another. Some of the challenges are inside us, as we feel superior to or less than other people. To live in balance and not based on emotions is an accomplishment that can take a lifetime.

Practices: Can you take an hour or a day and just be? Deep down, what is important to you? Look honestly and ask yourself, why do you do what you do?

Next Step: Be ready for changes in your life. Try not to take these changes personally.

Contemplate: Being non-attached does not mean disinterested.

Higher Octave: Be busy and involved, and non-attached at the same time.

Affirmation: I grow with every opportunity I meet in my life.

6 – THE LOVERS

Hindus believe that the Ganges' Divine waters purify those who immerse themselves in her. They have many rituals and procedures around immersion. Going into the cold water for a dip is exhilarating on many levels. The strong currents massage the body and teach ever-presence. I like to think of it as becoming one with the river.

Experience: Become One with the River

I have a friend in India who likes sitting by the Ganga River. She says she likes to sit where she can watch the current making little eddies, which show the current's flow pattern and give a sense of texture, with ripples, ebbs, and flows. Her routine used to be to take in the whole scene, including the dogs that stood on the shore and bathed in its fullness. One day, I suggested that she become one with the river instead.

Becoming one with the river means dropping the point of view of *I am looking at the river*. It means to make all of life a oneness, not a twoness. Two means "I" am having an experience. One means there is just the experience. No expectations, no right or wrong; the thought of better or worse completely disappears from the thinking and the body's sensations.

The Ganga River is a sacred natural part of India, but merging with the environment can happen for all of us anywhere. The local park becomes a sacred place when we bring this same attitude to it. Imagine watching a squirrel busy doing its daily tasks, gathering food and building a nest. Darting here and there, they are always mindful of what is around them. Become one with the squirrel.

Down at the ocean where seagulls fly up and down, sit on a dock and look around. They fly onto the sand, do some digging, then up into the sky again. They look so free! Can we imagine what it feels like to be them?

Can we do it with people? Join up with the ice cream man selling out of his cart in the park. We don't have to be close enough to hear him. We can feel what is said. The kids are running up to him with joyful anticipation. We can see the kids sitting and eating the ice cream too. We can imagine how, at the end of the day, the ice cream man goes home to Mrs. Ice Cream Man, takes out the garbage, and does his other chores around the house.

How about standing on the highway overpass and watching people in their cars driving home? The highway is like a river. We don't get to see the people for very long. In fact, we don't really see them at all. But we do see the cars. Can we join up with them on their journeys? Can we keep sight of them even after they pass? Remember, we are one with them; there is no lack of sight from an inner eye.

How about our partners? Can we become one with them? For me, being with a partner is a life of offering, giving, and willingness in each moment. What I receive is plenty. Giving in return is the only natural answer. I find this works with anybody—clients, shopkeepers, people I pass every day on my walks.

Become one with the rivers of life during your time on Earth. Break down your sense of separation and distinctions in your experiences. Since all of life is made of the same substances, there is no "other". There is only the *thinking* that there is other.

Jump into this river. Swim under the water for as long as you can. Feel the currents. Look to see all the life underwater. See how refreshing a swim is when you feel you're one with the river.

Significance: Gemini, seeing two as one, love, growth, new or conscious relationship, feeling full, combining two parts of ourselves, separation, loneliness, coexistence, varied interactions

Lessons: New relationships are wonderful, but is the outer relationship what we are really looking for? The Lovers teaches us that "relationship" is a symbol for something much deeper. The relationship we long for may be the one with *self*. Then all other relationships are possible.

Practices: Explore what keeps you apart from your experiences. Can you see your whole life as a river cruise? Think about people you know in your life and feel the compassion you have for them in their ups and downs.

Next Step: The next few people you meet—old friend or new, co-worker or family member—feel: *What can I give them?*

Contemplate: I am one with the river of life.

Higher Octave: I share with all whom I meet.

Affirmation: I am full, and able to be the lover I want.

5 – THE SHAMAN

Coming home from a walk the other night, I saw the Moon and Venus magnificently lit up by the Sun. The thought of the immense distance involved—that the light traveled hundreds of millions of miles across space to shine off of these planets and then down to me—almost knocked me over. When we contemplate the existence of the Universe and our place in it, many questions naturally arise.

Experience: Who's in Charge?

A young client recently wrote me, asking if I had an opinion on what she should do. She wrote that an opportunity suddenly came up for her to travel and take a course with a major teacher in her chosen field. She wondered if she should leave the month-long course that she was already attending in order to take the opportunity.

I suggested that she set aside the logistics (time, money, etc.), then feel what her intuition said. I also wrote in my response that her heart was big (she wanted to do it) and her will was weak (she was undecided). Who's in charge?

Variations of this type of indecision happen to all of us.

The mind says one thing, our feelings another, and the body wants what it wants. The parents say, "Good girls and boys *don't*...." Society says, "62.5 percent of the people *are*..." Media says, "For the *best-ever* experience..." How are we to know what to do?

So, we poll our friends looking for clarity. Some say left, some say right, some say left, then right, except for the ones who say right, then left. We ask our mate because they will tell us the truth, we hope. "Honey, you know I'll support, whatever you decide." Which direction is correct?

The closest thing to a universal truth I've found in my work is that we all enjoy being quiet in nature. The mind slows and problems disappear for a time. It's easy to believe that this mood change is due to nature, especially because the mind starts up again while walking back to the car. But we can also feel this same quiet at home while, say, meditating. Thus, nature cannot be the true cause (or at least, not the only).

What's going on?

Bees know to harvest nectar from flowers and bring it back to the hive. Watermelon seeds know when to germinate without any consulting, because they sense light and warmth. Leaves know to fall off trees in autumn, which protects the tree from freezing in winter and feeds the tree with nutrients released when the leaves decay on top of its roots. Can *we* live with that kind of clarity?

There is an essence inside us—the place of *knowing*, an inner voice. Our stories cannot be held there. It's a safe zone. When we live from this place, all our needs are satisfied. The mind stops running, and we see that it invents interpretations that make no sense. The body can have sensations, but they are not cause for action because they are seen for what they are: sensations. Our actions become more truthful because there is no need to do things that are not really beneficial. This is the place where all the questions disappear and answers magically appear.

Who's in charge? How are we to know what to do? Which direction is correct? What's going on? When I have questions—ones like at the beginning of this theme, whether they are consequential or non-consequential—I go to the quiet place inside me to "feel" the answer.

What do I want to eat? Should I take the class or not? There are no right or wrong answers, I just feel the truth for me in that moment. This way, I never have a question afterwards about my actions. This is the "who," of who is in charge for me—The *higher self*, the true Essence, consciousness.

When the *higher self* is in charge, questions and feelings come to peace, like sitting with a wise teacher or in beautiful nature. Everything else disappears. I don't feel a burden to know how things will work out, because I've come to trust everything as it is. I know that I am, but I do not know why. What peace this wisdom brings. All questions have disappeared.

Significance: Taurus, spiritual master, earth wisdom, transformation, big questions, navigating the currents, wisdom to know, self-doubt, insecurity, looking for answers

Lessons: We expend much effort trying to make sense of this world. When we let go of the idea of control, the natural flow provides. Shamen can make something out of nothing. We all can be teachers with the right heart and attitude. Seek inside and outside, then seek inside again.

Practices: How do you make decisions in your life? Practice viewing life as a bird sees it from high above. How does it feel when you realize you can't control your life or a particular situation?

Next Step: Take action knowing that there are no wrong actions.

Contemplate: I am willing to relinquish any need to be in charge.

Higher Octave: Life happens through me, not by me.

Affirmation: I trust and accept what is.

4 – THE PROVIDER

We are one world, one people, one family, one consciousness.

Experience: The Human Family

When we think of "the human family," memories of our own family of origin may come to mind. If we are fortunate, this family is composed of people who love us no matter what we do, people with whom we can let our hair down, people who accept us as we are.

Most families include uncles, aunts, grandparents, cousins, and in-laws. New extended families can include step-children and step-parents as people divorce and remarry.

Sometimes, close friends and mentors, neighbors, and pets become part of our family. In many cultures, the idea of the "nuclear" family has been expanded to include far more than blood relations.

Throughout human history, the supportive nuclear family shows up mostly in an economic environment of relative abundance, where basic survival is not at risk. Extended family provides economic and social support and stability.

The primary function of the family structure is procreation and the care and nurturing of human offspring. The nuclear family supports children's growth and development as they assume increasing responsibility in the broader culture.

Our knowledge and experience with family can help us understand communities because they often act like families. Communities, large or small, are social units with similar bonds. These bonds can stem from geographic proximity, common values, or shared interests. Newer kinds of communities can even be virtual.

Social ties within communities can be as important to our identity as the traditional/nontraditional family blood ties. We feel intense loyalty and duty to both community and family. Sports fans' ties to their teams can seem as strong as people's connections to church. Intentional community members live together, while a spiritual sangha prays together.

While procreation still usually occurs within the family, caring for children can extend beyond the family. As the saying goes, "It takes a village to raise a child." In all these ways, the same bonds of loyalty and kinship exist in communities as in families.

Communities can share beliefs, intentions, needs, goals, resources, and risks. There is a comradery between members of a community that, while perhaps not as intimate as a nuclear family, certainly can be as strong or stronger, especially later in life. Our bond to a teammate might feel stronger than our connection to a brother, sister, or cousin.

Perhaps the next level up for the human family is the nation. Nations share language, laws, culture, and much more. While at home in the nation, our citizenship may not seem like a big deal because everyone around us is from the same nation's family. But when we're halfway around the world and we meet someone from our own country who speaks the same language, we do feel a connection and an important bond.

Most modern nations have become so large and diverse that it can be a real challenge for citizens to find a common basis for community. This can lead to isolation and loneliness. Emphasis on borders, political parties, and power-based agendas can divide people more than unite them. But even in this context, examples of traditional national connection persist in groups like the Cherokee Indian Nation and the Huang in Asia. We can still look to these tribal nations as models as we work to revive connectedness in our human family.

Animals and plants also have families, as all living organisms are related. Our scientists have created an impressive classification system that shows the commonality between *species*, like a domestic cat, which then expands into the *genus,* which shows that cats include domestic cats and their cousins, leopards, tigers, lions, cougars, etc. The next classification up shows the *family* of all cats, called *Felidae*. The *order* for cats is called *carnivora*, which includes, cats, dogs, bears, and even weasels. The *class* for cats is mammals, and the *phylum* is vertebrates. Finally, we have the *animal kingdom,* including and connecting our house cat to all animals.

Plants belong to another kingdom.

Viewing all life this way lets us see the connectedness among all members of the family of living beings.

Let's look at the elements as shown in the Periodic Table of Elements. They have families, too. The tabular form of the table shows elements arranged by atomic number, electron configuration, and chemical properties. The rows show metals on the left and non-metals on the right; those are families. The vertical columns have similar physical or chemical characteristics of the outermost electron shell of their atoms in a core charge. The top element is used to describe a group, like the carbon or oxygen group. Element's abilities to merge and change make life possible. They support each other, which supports us. Gain more protons, and an element will morph into another element. How cool is that?

When we see life this way, the Earth is really inhabited by one BIG family. We depend on each other, no matter our classification. All our experiences and interactions from generation to generation keep the human family alive and vibrant. The basic elements, all animals and plants, even rocks, are in the human family. How do we know that? Because they feed and nourish us, they care for us, they tend to us, and they touch us.

As members of the human kingdom, we co-create ideas and share creativity with all our members, and our ideas and decisions have direct effects on the whole earthly family of animals, plants, rocks, and minerals.

We get inspiration from each other. What one starts, another one takes further. In the arts and sciences, or even house building or gardening, we are influenced by outside expressions. We create a family working on projects together, even if participants never meet. Similarly, we can think of all kids as our kids, because they are *humans'* kids or *creation's* kids.

Family means that we need to learn to see others as our kin. We need to be sensitive to others' needs. We must care for all, even if we call them other—human, plant, animal, and rock. We are all family—members of a planetary, galactic, and universal family.

How are we all connected? How can we understand life? Does our worldview include others' understandings? These questions disappear when we allow ourselves to be connected to all. We do well as individuals when all do well. We are kind of stuck with each other.

Family means so much more than just blood relationships. Opening the heart helps us feel each other. Family can be seen and felt within any relationship's dynamics. We need family to survive, and we can attain that anywhere, with anyone.

We feel separate, lonely, and less successful when we limit our efforts to material, worldly concerns. When we feel whole, we can't help but live according to an expanded definition of family. All are our brothers and sisters. Expectations and transactional ways of being drop away in a selfless love. Then we live in the one world family.

Significance: Aries, beginnings, strength that helps us grow, dynamic energy, overcoming challenges, living fully, family, getting the big picture, leaving adolescence, maturity

Lessons: Life provides all we need to grow. The structure of life itself can provide the nourishment we need. All of life conspires for us to be our best. That is the challenge and why we are here.

Practices: How can I be my best self? What would life be like if I felt connected to all? Does my worldview contain others?

Next Step: Practice gratitude for all that you have and don't have.

Contemplate: Life itself provides for every need.

Higher Octave: See yourself at your best, even when you aren't.

Affirmation: I trust the energies that flow through me.

75

3 – THE MIDWIFE

In a perfect world, we can overcome all challenges and love each other. We don't need to keep that a secret; we can live our lives from this belief out loud.

Experience: The Secret of Life

I heard a poignant short story a few years ago. The story goes like this: God asks Mrs. God, "Where should I hide the secret of life?" Mrs. God says, "Hide it in their heart, they'll never find it there."

The human heart, physically just an inch beneath the surface of our chest, is hard to access and even harder to open. When we say, "Open your heart," it isn't really the physical heart we are talking about. Otherwise, heart surgeons, while quite respected, might be considered Gods.

The metaphorical heart (the one referenced in the story) is a sacred, vulnerable place we have learned to protect and hide. When opened, it becomes a place where feelings are real and honored, without interpretation or prejudice. This place is always with us in silence and asks nothing of us. This heart is seen as "warm," and it grows stronger and warmer when fed with love and careful attention. People can sense when it flames, but the warmth it exudes never burns or stings to the touch.

We close and guard our hearts because we think that, by doing so, we protect ourselves from the world's dangers. We hide power and joy beneath the cover of unconscious actions and thoughts. We blame others when expectations are not met.

Experience is a great teacher when we see that we have locked the fox in the hen house, rather than locking it out. The fox is our avoidance, thoughts, and attitudes that cover real feelings. We think the fox will protect the chickens—our feelings—yet it eats them up. We close off soft, vulnerable opportunities that could touch us because we fear being overwhelmed. Then we engage in unnecessary drama as proof of the world's dangers, which require self-protection.

So, how do we find our heart-full, magical center? Simply put, love opens it naturally. Embodying love effortlessly melts our shields of fear. Loudly commanding the heart to open doesn't work. But all babies seem to be experts at it. Spend time in nature, be generous, be inviting, *be* and not *do*—this is what gets the heart's currents flowing.

In addition, I suggest spending time alone "pampering" yourself by appreciating who you are and what you offer. Give yourself gifts and take yourself on dates. Practice accepting yourself as you are. Allow yourself to feel vulnerable and experiment with vulnerability in interactions.

In these ways, we see how connected we are to everyone and everything. We see separation as the illusion it is. Yes, we have different bodies, but when we read heartbreaking stories of people's pain and grief halfway around the world, we feel it because we are connected in unseen ways.

Why is our heart magical? It's magical because when we live with an open heart, we feel all of life. We let go of small, self-protecting, unconscious thinking. It's one-stop shopping with the Divine—the Divine that is everything.

As a collective, we need to stop the painful games that separate us from the experiences we seek. We don't merely feel love, we *are* love. We *are* the heart. We have to stop believing the thoughts of the mind/ego because they are only out to protect *themselves*, not *us*. I guarantee that a short trip into the heart will be a beautiful journey, and the reward will be abundance and the secret of life.

Significance: Venus, integrity, heart opening, vulnerability, releasing judgements and comparisons, birth of the self, abundance, inner and outer wealth, love, wisdom

Lessons: It is time for rebirth and growth in one or more areas of life. The wise and calm Midwife is here to be of help every step of the way. She was born for this service. The more open and vulnerable we become, the more prosperity and possibilities will appear.

Practices: Calmly observe yourself, asking, Do I close my heart in some social situations? How do I do that? What do I feel when I allow myself to really be open? Reflect on your feelings of needing to love and to be loved.

Next Step: Start where you are. Be open to all life and all people, especially to those you resist.

Contemplate: There is nothing secret about love once you know it. You can see it in other people's eyes.

Higher Octave: The beauty you see in others is the beauty that is in you.

Affirmation: I give and receive love.

2 – THE YOGINI

The Chinese Buddhist deity, Kuan Yin, is the embodiment of compassion and mercy. She is often pictured in a posture of royal ease, radiating peace. She, who hears the cries of the world, has taken a vow to save all sentient beings. She sees all and knows all, embodying all that is important and inspiring to us.

Experience: The Knowing

There is a *knowing* centered near the gut, which is where the decisions of my life come from. It is who I am. I don't make any decisions with my mind anymore. I find the mind good for grocery lists and as a GPS, but the decisions I follow come from perceptions in my knowing. *Knowing* exists prior to the mind.

Of course, it wasn't always like this for me. I can't say when it or even how it changed— maybe fifteen years ago. But I do remember, on some of my foreign trips, coming to a place of needing to figure out what I wanted to do on a mundane level. When I had extra time, I could consider visiting a museum, shopping, or going to a temple. Or did I want to eat? But instead of thinking about my options, I felt I needed to sit still until I could feel an answer; I couldn't figure it out any other way.

Listening to that *knowing* inside me was the best, most prudent, accurate, and practical way to know what I felt or wanted. After that, I started applying this technique to my whole life.

This aspect of our *essence* is the *knowing*. It never makes a wrong decision because there are no wrong decisions. There are just decisions that are proper for this moment in time. The *knowing* knows because it is in the moment. Maybe it *is* the moment.

My mind had already become much quieter since a Vipassana ten-day meditation course in 1999. Once you are aware of the mind's game, the mind will obey. I give nighttime to the mind. At night, I let the mind do what it wants. But during the daytime, I'm hip to the mind, so I rarely get caught up in the crazy ideas that appear there.

The *knowing* is always with us. We access it without realizing it. A client asked me recently about developing his intuition. I showed him how he had already made some decisions by instinctively feeling the right answer. That is our *knowing*. How we get there is to have the discipline to let go of trying to figure out an answer, even releasing the need for an answer. Then the answer comes.

We can instantly recognize the rightness of answers from the *knowing*. This moment of *knowing* is a special gift. Not knowing, then *knowing*: this is really being alive.

"I know" this is of the mind. "I *know*" that is not the *knowing*.

Life teaches us that thinking we understand something often proves that we don't understand it at all. As we get older, this lesson is easier to learn.

We need to develop trust to access the *knowing*. Looking back at my early entry into the *knowing*, I see that I quieted the mind. Then I had a period of learning to trust what is.

I suggest learning to accept the seemingly unacceptable. We don't have to like the unacceptable or agree, but we might as well accept it. Trusting comes from realizing that there is a higher wisdom—what might be called natural laws—and a cosmic intelligence that is beyond our own limited thinking. When we can give up our arrogant belief that we know better, we open a door to trusting. Trusting helps us open ourselves to the *knowing*. These are some of the layers that need to be excavated to find our true nature.

Dear reader, I hope you can take this in. There is nothing to attain because the *knowing* is with you and is "your" *essence*. Life becomes about learning to listen better. We can turn off mental radio stations that get in the way of hearing our own heartbeat. We let go of pride and our need to be right. We dig below the inability to trust existence. There, the *knowing* lives, radiating wisdom full-time. Complete in itself, it is the wellspring of energy. Take time getting there. It is a friend to all, each and every moment. The *knowing* waits without any time constraints.

Significance: Moon, intuition, self-discovery, self-reflection, releasing arrogance, living in the moment, elegance, grace, one-pointedness, focus, increased confidence

Lessons: The life of the Yogini isn't lived at the highest while stuck in the ideas of the mind. The *knowing* is the crown jewel of opportunity that opens all doors. Enjoy the peace that comes from living with no guilt or obligation to live from the mind.

Practices: Have you had an experience of *knowing*? Do you use intuition in any aspect of your life? Experience arriving at the answer to a question by keeping quiet and tuning into the *knowing*.

Next Step: Near water, release anything that disturbs your feeling of peace.

Contemplate: I *know* that I *know* that I *know*.

Higher Octave: There is no agenda; there is nothing that must be done.

Affirmation: I live my life honoring the *knowing* inside me.

1 – THE MAGICIAN

Human consciousness can be calibrated on a 1 to 1000 logarithmic scale. Everything in the Universe radiates a frequency of energy that is permanent. By using the simple yes or no technique available with muscle testing, over years of research, David Hawkins was able to "calculate" levels of consciousness onto what he calls a Map of Consciousness.[1] I have personally found that understanding the frequency of certain attitudes and colors around me to be at the least freeing and at the best inspirational.

---

1   Hawkins, D. R., PHD (2017). *The Map of Consciousness Explained: A Proven Energy Scale to Actualize Your Ultimate Potential.* Hay House, LLC.

Experience: Feel the Force

From the moment I first talked by phone with my teacher, Curtis, many years ago, I knew he was someone special. Curtis said only three people knew what he could do and where to find him. He said I must have been blessed to have found one of those three people to guide me to him.

Curtis had much to share on many subjects that I wanted to explore. He is the most mystical, unique person I have ever met in a lifetime of traveling and spiritual seeking. He was born empathic with a photogenic and photographic memory. Any book I brought up, he had already read and could quote the section I referred to verbatim. He started studying Vedic astrology with his Vedanta master in Massachusetts when he was only fifteen years old.

He would quote dialog from movies to illustrate a point he made about the Enneagram (Ace of Gravity) or astrology (4 of Gravity). He wasn't particularly interested in having students; he said at the time that I was only the second person with whom he had shared his information.

A couple of months after our first phone conversation, I was blessed to attend two weeks of one-on-one mystery school with Curtis in magical Kauai, Hawaii. He taught me to observe the fullness of the moment, introducing me to the rich treasures to be found in the present. His way of being and his behavior slowed down time. He showed me how the Enneagram is visible in astrology, in combinations of planets that are imprinted on us at birth. The Enneagram is the mother archetype, and the astrology chart is like a photograph or an X-ray of what the archetype looks like.

These were mind-blowing, awakening days, and a time of complete restart in my life. We discussed the houses of the astrology horoscope sitting on a Hawaiian beach where we could view almost the whole visible sky, horizon to horizon. We watched a slowly setting Sun's dramatic array of saturated colors as the sky eventually evolved to its eternal darkness. We became one watching an ocean and horizon that went on forever. As the sky ultimately filled with stars, I felt that they had all come out for us on this particularly dark night. We sat there a long time discussing more mystical subjects.

Curtis loved to teach in marketplaces where he invited me to watch people express their personality through their manner of walking and dress. Arm movements and pace have meaning. He showed me how the personality "radiates" from within the body, and he taught me how to "feel" it.

His intuition was so powerful that just standing next to him increased my own. Being with him for two weeks changed my life. I left Hawaii on a real high, headed to India, deeply appreciative for those incredible experiences.

The Star Wars empire introduced many of us to the idea of "the Force." In one memorable scene, as Luke struggles to lift his ship from a swamp using his new skills, Yoda says, "For my ally is the Force, and a powerful ally it is. Life creates it, makes it grow. Its energy surrounds us and binds us. Luminous beings are we, not this crude matter. You must feel the Force around you; here, between you, me, the tree, the rock, everywhere, yes. Even between the land and the ship." [1]

What wisdom those entertaining films have brought to young and old for generations!

Yoda ends up lifting Luke's ship out of the water because Luke does not yet have the power to do it himself.

In physics, force changes the behavior of objects in space and time. This force is also called energy. Force is physical energy and intensity. Just as we can move an object with physical force, we can exercise power, influence, or authority over people with more subtle kinds of force. This force is around us and within us. Newton and Einstein made great advances in understanding, labeling, and quantifying the forces in and around us.

In my teacher, Curtis, I met a real-life Yoda. He said to me in the marketplaces, "Young Luke, feel the Force" (though I was about ten Earth years older than he). This was how he went about sharing something that was so completely instinctive to him.

An alchemist and a magician, Curtis showed me how to make something from nothing by using what is called magic, but what is really happening on a higher, non-physical frequency of vibration that we feel but can't see. The lower frequencies of the physical realm run according to the physical plane's own natural laws. But, experiences of the higher frequencies of love, peace, joy, reverence, or serenity can blow our mind, when they are simply operating according to their own natural laws.

While it's easy to associate force with something that someone does to us, there is no reason we can't use forceful energy for our own high purpose. We can learn to trust and feel our own natural energy—our force—but not by manipulating it like Star Wars characters. It's about becoming conscious of what is already there.

As implied in the hip phrase, "I feel you," this energy can help us communicate more deeply. When we understand force, we get clear about the vastness of the playing field of life. It includes what you feel but don't see. Then life becomes an opportunity to witness how all-encompassing we can become. The energy we feel in any moment reaches beyond the physical plane.

Humans radiate energy like all living organisms; it's another law of physics. Many feel this energy as people's happiness or sadness. When one gets accomplished at reading this

---

1   Lucas, G. (Director). (1980). *Star Wars: Episode V - The Empire Strikes Back* [Film]. Lucasfilm.

energy, it's possible to know what others are thinking. We can learn to observe and use the energy generated around us to sense attitudes, expectations, judgments, and more.

We can also learn to observe our own behavior and thinking, and to tune into our own force. This is the secret to living a conscious life. To accomplish this, one needs to feel energy—the force in and between all organisms. The transformation comes when we add our own energy to the forces we feel. We can't take what happens in life personally because it creates a story that makes us feel unfocused. Take what happens around us for what it is: a reflection of wisdom's power to support our becoming more conscious, as if by magic.

"Feel the Force" translates to, "Be aware of the limiting thought forms contained in what people say and do around us, including within our *self*." There are so many subtle codes being telegraphed each moment. It's like the ultimate detective novel. One might say it sounds boring. I say, give it a try.

Everything turns out well for Luke, Yoda, and Obi. It *is* Hollywood, after all. How it will turn out for you, dear reader, is the concern. Recognize the limitations of believing our thoughts and actions. Recognize that these realizations can help initiate change. Recognize that everyone is and has force, and that we can feel and learn from that force.

Significance: Mercury, beginnings, being open, higher frequencies, the higher self, power of positive thinking, concentrated mastery, creativity, self-expression, manifesting

Lessons: We have no choice but to start where we are. As we gain perspective and learn to recognize the energy around us, life becomes clearer. We deal with energies all day that we cannot see: emotions, feelings, anger, and fear. The individual who can change themselves is the one who is a Magician.

Practices: Start to notice your inner reactions to the energy people express around you. Notice how different your body's energy is when you are happy or when you're sad. Close your eyes on a bus or train, during a conversation with friends, or at a restaurant, and notice what you feel.

Next Step: Take a walk in beautiful nature and see if magic appears.

Contemplate: I can fulfill my own destiny.

Higher Octave: Release the self-appointed duties of being the one to judge, correct, control, direct, and change the world.

Affirmation: I trust what I feel but can't see.

0 – THE FOOL

When we use the mind to understand life, life doesn't always make sense. The keys to understanding life may be confusing and point in different directions towards the same goal. The small self makes no sense of this. The higher self views life above the haze.
The best part is: we have the ability to choose.
But that doesn't mean we make choices with clarity.

Experience: Life is Counterintuitive

Let's look at the word "sense." It can mean a mental faculty through which we apprehend the external world. So, our sense of "sense" appears in our mind.

But sense can also mean a conscious awareness, a sense of style, a sense of danger, or a gut feeling. This is instinct- or intuition-based sense.

Our ancient ancestors were more profoundly connected with nature than we are now, deeply trusting intuition to guide their lives. They lived with the flow of nature and the seasons leading their way, with no need to question or to understand life.

But today in modern society, conditioned by 5,000 years of thinking inherited from family and society, most of us unthinkingly rely on a mental sense of rationality to define, judge, and make sense of most aspects of our lives. We use our logic to measure life and its events.

We believe so much in our own logic. Yet the people we know and trust may be using a logic completely different from ours. They may judge our logic as illogical! Ironically, conflicts like this often show up with our mates and those closest to us. Why is this? Well, I'm not sure, but I do know it's one example of how life can be counterintuitive.

Our internalized rationalism often has rigid rules, insisting life should work a certain way. But life has a frustrating way of side-stepping our rules.

Sometimes we must go north to go south. We steer a sailboat by pushing the tiller in the opposite direction of our intended course. Sometimes, the most productive thing one can do is sleep. We try to figure out a math problem, then the answer comes when we aren't thinking about it. We push on what we want, but it stays just beyond our eager grasp, only coming to us when we ease off and stop trying so hard. This is how a counterintuitive approach shows up and helps us succeed in daily life.

More examples abound. Sometimes, we need to stop moving to find the way forward. When we stop studying, we might learn more. We stop knocking, and the door opens. We slow down, but win the race. We learn more in silence than by speaking. We are seen when we're quiet, and ignored when acting out.

How does intuition fit into this picture? We must release our thinking and embrace our feelings to navigate the narrow channel of our intuitive being.

I use this in my spiritual life by easing off the idea "I know better." We can burn out by trying too hard in meditation. We can get blown up by following a drastic diet regimen or by being too ascetic. By judging others, we may feel we've risen above their behavior, only to catch ourselves behaving the same way.

The Bible teaches that the meek shall inherit the earth, the last shall be first, and to turn the other cheek when struck. St. Francis of Assisi said to give is to receive, to console is to be consoled. When we're young, we look forward to the wisdom of advanced age, but when we finally get old, we come to the truth that we know very little. In this counterintuitive moment is the freedom to know everything.

Perhaps life works this way because we keep using our sense of mind in a futile effort to figure life out. Somehow, we come to trust our sense of rationality, compounding it with conditioned thinking and an inability to assume the long view. Rationality makes it reasonable to choose a direction or an action that can almost guarantee we won't receive what we want. But in fact, what we're chasing might not be good for us, might not be attainable, or may not even be the thing we desire. I suggest we learn to back off, let life take over, and live with the flow of life, letting things come when they come.

We are a complex species. Sometimes we face outward, asserting ourselves in some areas of life, while in others we're inward facing. For example, in work situations we are confident, but in a one-on-one social setting we find it hard to act naturally. We can win a Nobel Prize in physics, but feel all thumbs when making a simple painting or drawing. We can be a total daredevil until we are asked to care for a rose bush, change a diaper, cook a meal, or give a speech. When operating in our natural state, things simply are; Counterintuitive things don't seem so, well, *counter*. Sometimes we really need to go north to get south.

We are composed of a variety of attitudes and skills. The way through the maze is to know that we may not know. Counterintuitive is sometimes the way of life.

Significance: Finding one's way, we don't always know, truth, foolishness, independence, trust, freedom, heart's truth, courage, change, new opportunity

Lessons: The Fool believes only what he sees with his head. A higher wisdom is guiding the way. It is foolish not to follow this wisdom, but we learn this inch by inch over a lifetime.

Practices: Can you see examples from your life when using your habitual ways of thinking was not the best course? Can you see examples in your life where others thought you were a little crazy? Stop and *feel* when making decisions. Ask yourself, does it *feel* right?

Next Step: Go with the flow. Don't let ideas in the mind influence what you feel.

Contemplate: "What a fool believes, he sees; No wise man has the power to reason away." [1]

Higher Octave: I trust life and the powers that have manifested this sacred moment.

Affirmation: I will make myself small in order to be large.

---

1   The Doobie Brothers. (1978, August). What a Fool Believes (K. Loggins & M. McDonald, Eds.)

[Album, Nightwatch What a Fool Believes]. Warner Bros.

THE TEACHERS

LIVING ENERGY

Wherever we go, we carry stuff with us. The backpacks we carry on the road of life have ways of becoming part of us when we let them. But we are not turtles carrying only our homes—places of security and comfort. Instead, we also carry limitations, shame, fear, and anger that block living energy. Let's repack our loads.

Experience: Bring it Back

It is common to want to emulate the aspects, traits, and skills of people we admire. From their style of dress, to their friendliness, assertiveness, patience, calmness, or a fiery confidence and motivation, we notice others and wish to be like them. This yearning can also expose our own insecurities. We might wonder why we lack these characteristics or why we are not more like our friends. We might go straight to a belief that we aren't good enough.

We get stuck when we envy what others have; often deluding ourselves into believing that we'll never be like them.

The last few years I have noticed within me an amazing ability to assimilate the qualities of others. I say "amazing" because I did not have this ability before. I see a quality in someone else, and absorb it into me by becoming it, expressing it, and then developing it further.

In sessions with my clients, I started calling this phenomenon "bring it back." "Bring it back" means admiring qualities in others and then learning to adapt the characteristics to our own ways of being.

Instead of competing, this is a way we can learn from and support each other. Bring back a skill or quality that you see in others. Bring it back to yourself. We can even do this with skills we already have by expanding the breadth of that skill.

For example, let's say that we are outgoing and communicative in one-on-one social settings, but go quiet in larger social situations. I'm suggesting that we can learn to bring back social skills in larger settings, adding it to our core personality. We may find it easier to communicate in a relaxed setting, but we can bring back someone else's skills when socializing in public circumstances and feel just as comfortable.

Do you admire qualities in people you see on TV or in the media? Bring it back. From the Dalai Lama to Oprah, or even your favorite weatherman. If you want to be helpful like a worker at your grocery store, bring it back. Appreciate the honesty and sincerity of a coworker and bring it back.

In order to do this, we have to be open—to release our insecurities or see through them. We can use the admiration we feel like a pole to help us vault over our insecurities.

In my own experience, I think my new skill came when I gained the ability to see past my own perceived limitations. So much comes from this ability to quietly and effortlessly, let go.

We must do this from a quiet mind with a feeling of inner assurance. It helps to appreciate that person. Use that wonderment as a vehicle for growth. I use my appreciation of someone's quality as an inducement—an encouragement to leap over the pain of my vulnerability in order to take on a new skill.

I suggest we try this slowly at first. Copy a painting technique from a friend or master, pick up cooking tips from the newspaper or social media, or follow advice from self-help books and gurus. Make a conscious effort to grow and change. As we gather confidence and speed, it becomes easier to acquire new skills. Like the little engine that could, bringing it back can help propel us up the steep hills of life.

Significance: The fiery aspect of fire, moving forward, concentration, self-acceptance, doubt, changes, charisma, confidence, leadership, pessimism, creativity, becoming natural

Lessons: Living Energy encourages us to be active and dynamic in growth. Everything is an opportunity when we view life that way. Be ever-appreciative and open.

Practices: Name some qualities you would like to be able to express. Can you sense what keeps you from attaining these qualities? Tell the people around you what you admire about them.

Next Step: Start to bring back special qualities from others around you and make them your own.

Contemplate: Is the glass half full or half empty?

Higher Octave: Everything around me, "good" or "bad," is an opportunity to expand into consciousness.

Affirmation: I can float like a butterfly, be like a bee, and have my nose ready to gather pollen everywhere.

LOVING ENERGY

In many cultures, spider webs symbolize patience, creativity, and the interconnectedness of all things. They are often seen as a symbol of balance, harmony, and the delicate yet intricate nature of life.
The balance we want to find in loving energy is to be open to what life is offering us each moment. Connectedness is a gift of life that supports us always. Everything is connected. No matter where we go, there we are. It doesn't expire; it doesn't need days or nights off.
It's always holding us close.

Experience: Synchronicity

Have you ever had a situation like this? I think we all have.

There is something you want to do or some place you want to go to. Or maybe there is a mate with whom you want to connect. You waffle indecisively between your head and your heart for days, weeks, and years until the Universe tries to settle the dispute for you.

Let's say I want to quit my job to follow my dream of being a chef, but I have held myself back, frozen on the precipice of a leap. One day while driving, I'm thinking about being a chef, when a song comes on the radio. Voices sing, "It's your thing, do what you wanna do."[1] Then, people next to me in the grocery line start talking about how much they admire a chef on a magazine cover. The next day, a co-worker tells me enthusiastically about their relative who is starting culinary school.

After three or more such events—some may call them coincidences—I mention these experiences to a good friend who knows of my dilemma. This wise friend might tell me that's called synchronicity; it's how the Universe talks to us, nudging us to act.

We may not have heard of synchronicity before, so the little nuanced messages often slide right past us while we fail to consider the Universe's interest in us.

But when bread crumbs keep leading directly to the path we *know* is right, even if it is really frightening, we gradually gain the inner energy necessary to overcome our fear of the unknown. We can become a roaring lion who would rather die trying than live without giving our all. The seesaw tips and we slide into our new direction. We know it's the right thing to do.

Synchronicity is the concept that everything is related, even if we can't see a connection. It is defined as "the simultaneous occurrence of events which appear significantly related but have no discernible causal connection."[2]

Carl Jung coined the term synchronicity almost one hundred years ago but the concept wasn't new. The idea of synchronicity is depicted in one of my favorite symbols—Indra's Net (can you guess why it's a favorite?), which first appeared in the Atharva Veda in India around 1100 BCE, five hundred years before Buddha's birth.

Modern author Francis Cook describes Indra's Net this way:

"Far away in the heavenly abode of the great god Indra, there is a wonderful net which has been hung by some cunning artificer in such a manner that it stretches out infinitely in all directions. In accordance with the extravagant tastes of deities, the artificer has hung a single glittering jewel in each "eye" of the net, and since the net itself is infinite in

1   The Isley Brothers. (1969). It's Your Thing. On It's Our Thing [Audio File]
2   Jung, C. (1960). *Synchronicity: An Acausal Connecting Principle.* Princeton University Press.

96

dimension, the jewels are infinite in number. There hang the jewels, glittering "like" stars in the first magnitude, a wonderful sight to behold. If we now arbitrarily select one of these jewels for inspection and look closely at it, we will discover that in its polished surface there are reflected *all* the other jewels in the net, infinite in number. Not only that, but each of the jewels reflected in this one jewel is also reflecting all the other jewels, so that there is an infinite reflecting process occurring."

Each jewel contains the interconnected whole of existence. But our separate bodies sometimes seem to suggest the opposite—that independent, separate parts come together to make up the whole. Each jewel is in flux, being upgraded each moment into a new jewel, like the body is continually refreshing cells. In the same way, the present moment contains flux, always becoming the next moment. The internet is a modern example of Indra's Net.

Life feels like it contains many other levels of existence that are too subtle for our normal awareness. But there are nearer levels, just over the next hill, that we can relate to and feel, even if they are invisible to our eyes. Once we open to this possibility, anything is possible, and synchronistic events are more likely. From the mind's point of view, it can seem like synchronicity has an on/off switch. Sometimes we notice it, while other times, we don't see it, so we think it must not be happening. But synchronicity is always operating. The ability to acknowledge it comes from our perspective and viewpoint of life in each moment.

We can be open to the flow of life. We can also be closed by keeping our focus small and narrow. Is there a way to live open more of the time? How do we find, then stay, in this energy space? We need to learn to live less in the mental and emotional world, busy and distracted by our needy personalities. Instead, relax into a more intimate relationship with life—heartful, open to intuition, looking to see what's there. The more we open to synchronicities, the more we'll see that they never stop. Everything starts taking on meaning. We get used to the *ah!* moments. Each *ah!* may not be as big every time, but we expect them, rather than being surprised by their appearance.

We can explain synchronicity as existence on a higher level of consciousness. But also, Indra's Net shows us that all things are connected. Both accounts of synchronicity are accurate. Synchronicity comes when you are seeing at a higher level of vibration—a frequency where everything is connected. There, everything is in synchronicity. On this level, no cause exists as everything affects everything else. Then we are in the flow of energy, where limited definitions disappear and the oneness of all reveals itself.

Significance: Watery aspect of fire, expansion, flow, self-knowledge, openness, challenges, growth, freedom, satisfaction, smallness, disharmony, stagnation, closed, accomplishment, ambition

Lessons: We can make our own "good luck" by being open to what is. Loving Energy knows that seeing challenges as opportunities is how to make things happen. Living this way, moment-to-moment, is our highest potential.

Practices: Do you have examples of synchronicity working for you in your life? Can you feel the life that is more than just what you can see? What is your attitude toward living this way?

Next Step: If something is possible, then assume it will happen without concern for "when".

Contemplate: Do I sabotage my own expressions? If so, how?

Higher Octave: Feel gratitude for the moment as it is.

Affirmation: I create my own future.

RELEASING ENERGY

There is an old saying, "The squeaky wheel gets the grease," which means that someone who complains or causes problems is more likely to receive attention or help than someone who stays quiet.
On a wheel, it's easy to see that consistent use causes the need for oil. What's less obvious is the cause of our own squeaking wheels and how we can apply oil to them.

Experience: Triggers

When we become an expert in something, a hobby or a profession, there are small, subtle skills that make a difference in our proficiency. The phrase "tricks of the trade" comes to mind. I'm thinking of the weekend golfer who watches YouTube videos, reads magazines, and talks to other golfers out on the links, all to pick up one or two special tips to improve their game. Knitters talk to other knitters, cooks look for nuances from everyone to add to their offerings, and gardeners love to connect with other gardeners, even in winter, to better their efforts.

In the game of waking up to who we really are, our triggers are tools that can add to our insights and improve our practice of presence. Triggers are a spur or provocation that take us out of the moment and lead us on a neurological cascade of thoughts and fantasy, often amplifying the ego's fears and insecurities. However, as we understand and observe them, we find that triggers give us a unique opportunity to end the false stories we live in, freeing us from the confusion caused by mental chatter and compulsive reactions.

We are in the moment, content with what is, and then we get triggered. Someone says something that sets us off. Suddenly, we react from a program of unconscious behavior designed to overcome the feelings arising from the triggering. And it's beneath our awareness.

When we are triggered, our life feels distorted. We can't trust the mind because it comes up with crazy ideas not based on fact. We also can't trust our feelings because they are overly sensitive and inaccurately interpret scenarios. We can't even trust our actions because they are often compulsive.

Once triggered, we have a litany of programmed behaviors that cascade, like the operating system on our computers. Only we can stop them, and we do so by observing our behavior and coming back to presence.

This is not something that happens on the first attempt. I'll be honest with you—it may take decades. It may take the rest of your life.

But we can make progress right away. It takes effort to be aware of our own behavior and patterns. Having a partner or friend to point things out can help, but life (the guru that life is) itself will act in ways to reflect our actions back to us. We need to be open enough to see life at work.

Some real-world examples will help clarify this. We are racing to arrive at an important appointment and the light turns red. We yell at the light, yell at the other drivers on the road, or light up yet another cigarette. Someone we respect says in an innocent conversation that they don't like the color red because it makes people look overweight. We think of all the red in our closet, immediately stop talking, and look for a place to hide. Someone says something impolite about our post on social media and we either blame them for their bad judgment or don't post again for weeks. Our mate wants a divorce from our unhappy marriage, and we react by lashing out.

These triggers touch the places where we hold our insecurities. The reactions are unconscious, programmed, and nearly invisible to us, but are often clear to others who know us well.

The triggers aren't our problem. The triggers are neutral. Our reactions to them can be problematic because the reactions arise from having expectations. Still, triggers can become our friends. It is beautiful how they come up and we react. We react because we have a stuck place. I'm thinking of that squeaky wheel. This is why we react to our triggers. Our limitations rub up against life, making us act in unconscious ways.

The lubricants for this action are knowledge and awareness of our reactions. When we can see beyond our reactions, our "wheels" become less dry and noisy.

Experience your triggers with openness and vulnerability. When we are triggered, we are not vulnerable. Vulnerability is open; triggered is hurting and closed off.

We have let go of reactions from childhood. Insecurities in our teens are healed by growth and life experiences. Behaviors from our twenties and thirties disappear in our forties and fifties. We might bring some of them with us, of course. Something must be the last behavior we shed before we pop —before we become free of our triggers, move to Costa Rica, or die.

Let's be ever-conscious of our actions! Let's give ourselves love and grace in the knowledge that we do the best we can at all times. Let's remember that we get triggered and use that experience as a tool for our highest evolution.

Significance: Airy aspect of fire, thinking that stops flow, trust, acceptance, fulcrum, leaving impressions, competitive, bossy, impulsive, adjustments, long-term view, facing challenges

Lessons: Releasing Energy has youthful strength on its side. In life, we come to learn that the ways we act have meaning. We can't just bulldoze everything in our path. Checking in before acting helps everyone involved in the end.

Practices: What triggers you? How do you handle those triggers? Learn to watch others in your life as they get triggered, and see how they respond.

Next Step: Learn to smile and laugh when you are triggered. This will oil your noisy wheels.

Contemplate: I am only as strong as my weakest reaction.

Higher Octave: All of life helps me to grow strong and free.

Affirmation: I let life go like water rolling off a duck's back.

OBSERVING ENERGY

Life is full of little miracles—the unexpected coincidences that bring appreciation and joy. They can appear out of the least expected places or experiences. We can learn to expect the unexpected.

Experience: It's the Little Things

The little things in life and relationships can become the juiciest parts, particularly as we get older. When we are young, everything is important and sensitive. Later, as life slows down, special moments are like rests between the notes in music. They give us rhythm, which supports life's harmony.

When we are young, we work to assert our will. How much will people notice me? How can I let people know I'm cool? Or the other side of the coin: I'll disappear because being invisible is safer. I'll act out again because I am sure to get some attention.

In the middle years, life can be a bit of a no-man's land. We don't yet appreciate ourselves or what we do. So, it's hard to appreciate (or remember to appreciate) the mate, the kids, the work, the life. That's a lot of things needing attention. No wonder we start getting stomach aches, back pain, and headaches!

Later, we are ready to smell the roses and enjoy life's rewards. Still, at this time, life can be confusing. Making bread for someone we care about starts becoming a better experience than eating the bread. We don't mind looking for the missing car keys again. We find our mate's annoying habits cute.

But don't get stuck by the age constraints I am suggesting. Wisdom can set in at any age. We can all appreciate the piles of dirty laundry worn during a hard workweek. We can all give the end of a fresh loaf away to the humblest of beings. We can all enjoy a special meal on an ordinary day.

Squeeze a hand, share a sweet smile, smell a flower, or make a surprise to brighten someone's day.

I suggest that spiritual practices like yoga and meditation need to be experienced off the mat, not just on the mat. Yoga means "union" and can mean unifying all the different parts of our lives. Meditation practice teaches us to quiet the mind even when life gets frenzied. Let's take these practices into everyday life. We do this by connecting with everything we meet and silencing the mind throughout the day. Don't limit love making to physical acts in the bedroom. Try making love with life in the living room or kitchen by adding subtle acts of love into your daily life. Do unto others as we wish them to do unto you.

One of life's counter-intuitive realities is that predictable experiences often go underappreciated, as we have expectations. Unexpected events can bring out more gratitude because we don't have expectations. Notice the small things in life and watch how appreciation grows.

Significance: The earthy aspect of fire, grounding, finding center, communication, focus, self-esteem, personal freedom, judgments, suffering, faith in self, coming into balance

Lessons: Observing Energy has a simple message to share. Find gratitude and appreciation in everything that happens. With the right attitude, frowns turn into smiles.

Practices: List some special things about someone dear to you. List some small things that someone would appreciate about you. Do a small, sweet thing for a stranger today.

Next Step: Find some small, beautiful things that happen around you each day.

Contemplate: The more grounded I am, the more I appreciate my life.

Higher Octave: Being willing to express enthusiasm can help overcome our greatest fears.

Affirmation: I will release my shadows until they find peace.

LIVING FLOW

Most people recognize the puzzle parts—thoughts, fears, experiences, dreams—that comprise their life.
We can see them individually, but the trick becomes to fit them together into a whole, integrated, happy, conscious picture we call self.

Experience: Identity

The concept of identity within the conscious awakening process is extremely important to understand. However, it's not easy to understand, nor is it easy to make the changes this understanding encourages.

Let's start by looking at Merriam-Webster Dictionary's definition:

Identity is "the distinguishing character or personality of an individual." This is the broad view of ourselves that we show the world—our "lower self".

At three months of age, we grab our foot. We don't know it's a foot or that it's *our* foot because we haven't learned concepts yet. But conditioned learning is ongoing as we experience the world and figure out ways to make sense of it. A common first identity of a very young person is that of Daddy's or Mommy's "good" little girl or boy. This one can stay with us our whole life.

As we grow, the identities we adopt are ways to express our personalities, images, and ideals. We think that this is the way of life, and it is for some people. In school, we are the athlete, the academic, the comedian, the popular one, the artist, the lackey, etc.

Over time, these mold into the adult identities that we can put on and take off like costumes hanging in our closet: the parent, the helper, the business mogul, the sophisticate, the charmer, the nomad, the spinster. The need to take on a strong identity as a young adult is really the fortification of a strong ego. Oftentimes, we are taught that if we show up as "ME" then our chosen paths in life become easier. We are also consciously and unconsciously covering our insecurities by creating value in our identity for the rest of the world.

At work, we are the "strong, capable, overachiever." We stress about work because we don't want anyone to know the truth—one we barely share with ourselves. We fear that we are not as capable as we let on. So, we work extra hours and forego a social life.

In our social life, we have terrible relationships. We control them by picking loser mates that we pretend to love because the feeling of being appreciated, no matter how disingenuous it is, is like a gentle summer breeze to cool the heat of strong self-doubts (or maybe just the fear of being alone and unlovable). We identify ourselves as the "deeply loving mate".

With parents, we take on the role of the bumbling adult child or the caretaker, either reverting to our seven-year-old selves every time we are on the phone with them, or running to help at their every beck and call.

But when the pulls of money and status, appearances, travel, high society (or even low society), and achievement have us suffering in pain and disillusionment, we look to find what is real. And that is where we start looking at our identities.

We think that these outward-facing identities are who we are, but they are only a façade—an illusory image. They're not who we are. They're not living in the moment, and they aren't in integrity. They're roles we play. They're strategies. They are our compulsions and obsessions.

So how do we surrender our identity? First, we need to take them on and own them. Then, we can release them. When we identify our common behaviors, we can see through the underlying needs and let them go. Identity is attractive at the extreme ends of personhood, the polarities. When we are feeling out of balance and lost, we happily take on the identities. In the centered middle, we can more easily let them go.

We have to slow down enough to see the story and realize that we carry this energy around with us—that we live and act from it. We have to fully own it and see all of its light and dark edges. We have to own the suffering it can bring, and then we have to curse it—to hate it—even if just for a moment, so that we may empty out all our feelings and experiences. This is catharsis. At many points in time, it served us to be this way—to have and use this identity as a front—until it doesn't serve us anymore.

Then, we want to release it. We see it contains untruth. We stop feeling good doing it. We know everyone else can see through our behavior. We may still harbor some of the same behaviors after we release the identity, but we are not attached to them.

When we release our identity, we release any holds it had over us. We even release our own perceived limitations. We will come to love our *self* as we are.

In the same way we identify with personalities, we often identify with the events of the world. When "bad" things happen, like weather, or a flat tire, we take it personally, as if we caused it or deserve it. Then comes the feeling that more bad things will happen. Instead, when we look from a larger perspective, we can come to know that other people's attitudes towards us are not our concern. We can see things happen *for* us, not *to* us.

Who are we really? Well, we are that slow, deep-breathing one who appears relaxed in nature. We are the one that is content with quiet and space and needing nothing else. In our quiet moments, there are no thoughts of anything else. We are the one that is left when all the identities are released, the one who has no need for an identity. We become the eternal one who, in that one full moment, knows all and has experienced all and has no need for anything other than the complete WHOLENESS of right here, right now. In the absence of all the identities, we are nothing and everything.

The capable worker, the doubtful partner, and the adult child are roles we identify with because we feel we need a solution to the learned "you are an I" mantra. Who we really are, underneath all the misidentifications of identity, is an underlying Essence. This Essence needs nothing and has everything. The body needs food and shelter, the Essence needs nothing. Thinking otherwise is also a misidentification.

Take it slow, dear ones. All this is a little like doing electrical repair with the electricity on. It requires great focus, or we might get zapped. We need to get a perspective on the self to view the identifications properly. Knowing how to work on the identity while also being in the identity is a challenge. We may need to adopt a squinty-eyed look at our self to see the roles that we play. I suggest an all-out war by REMEMBERING who you really are. It takes willingness, time, and love—loving the self and the life—to shed our personas.

Significance: The fiery aspect of water, self-awareness, deep dive, floating, relationship with self, confusion, emotionality, uncentered, doubtful, building confidence, connection

Lessons: Living Flow teaches us that relationship with others begins with the relationship to self. Assurance about the self comes from seeing the parts as they are. Being whole helps us remain steadfast in the winds of life.

Practices: Explore the different personas you have used in your life. How do you act when you get emotional and angry? Have you experienced the quiet self in nature or at any other time?

Next Step: Learn to observe your behavior, not just act the behavior.

Contemplate: Holding positions and identities makes it harder to be the true *self*.

Higher Octave: Being the same with everyone can become effortless.

Affirmation: I recognize my *self* for who I am.

LOVING FLOW

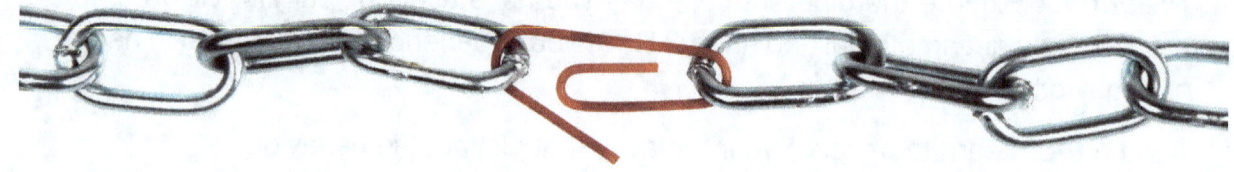

*Our weakest links are our vulnerabilities.
If we hide from them in shame or fear, we see them as failures or
challenges. But if we think of them as feedback—as homework,
a super workout, or steps the boss wants us to take before our next
raise/promotion at work—then they can become strengths. We learn
to work with them and love them and ourselves, all at the same time.*

Experience: Vulnerability

Life is full of vulnerability. We can't live without air, water, or food for very long. We can die at any moment from a natural or manmade event. In the face of these vulnerabilities, many of us seek to protect ourselves. You can likely see it in your everyday behaviors.

We protect ourselves from events, thoughts, and feelings that we perceive as physically or emotionally overwhelming (or even harmful), by not allowing ourselves to move through them (or them through us).

One of the most common ways I see clients protect themselves is to close their hearts. Closing the heart means building a barrier to ward off ideas and feelings that are painful to feel and see. Often, these feelings arise when we confront our own insecurities and limitations.

Much of this starts in early childhood when we are, in fact, quite vulnerable and unable to defend and care for ourselves. We unconsciously protect ourselves from feeling the full impact of any painful ongoings around us. Different personalities will find different methods of achieving this same goal.

In our twenties, as we navigate adult life, these strategies become second nature. They feel inbred, as if they are a natural part of us. When we let them go, it can feel like losing part of our self.

The inherent vulnerability of life and our protective mechanisms go hand in hand. Every time we open the door to leave our house, we undergo micro changes. Urban people might use the term "putting on your armor". We do not know what will happen in the wild, so our body responds to defend against the unknown.

Our closed hearts are particularly apparent in relationships, especially intimate ones. They can feel like jousting contests in which no one allows themselves to be seen. Both parties exert effort to minimize painful feelings—their own and their partners.

Allowing ourselves to be vulnerable is like taking an ancient remedy for what ails us. We feel worlds better afterwards. But it's also like swimming in a lake with cold water. It takes some getting used to. Vulnerability helps us feel closer to others because we drop our feelings of separation. Our self-image improves as we find it easier to love ourselves.

So, what is being vulnerable? Some examples include admitting what you feel emotional about, admitting that you could have done better in a situation, saying things you're scared to say or that you don't know how to say, and admitting you need help. However, intention matters. When we do these things to impress other people, or to be noticed or appreciated, it isn't vulnerability as much as acting out a role. This is not honest or open behavior.

The key to true vulnerability is to live with an open heart. When we stop trying to protect our heart from intimidating feelings, we can live a more open and vulnerable existence.

The mind may say being vulnerable is weakness, but from what I have seen, most people prefer to be around others who are vulnerable. In many ways, it is viewed as a strength. Being around vulnerable friends, family, and partners is more real—honest, authentic, open, transparent, and sincere. When we surround ourselves with people who are comfortable with their vulnerability, it invites us to feel confident in our vulnerability as well.

I suggest we strive to be vulnerable—able to express what is on and in the heart. Speak from the heart, but not the one connected to the head—the one that wants instead of feels. Let's dissipate the veneer of the personality that covers who we really are. When we can observe the micro actions inside us, we begin to shed that toughened layer.

Significance: The watery aspect of water, authentic, honest, emotional, sensitive, hurt and pain, deceptions, integrity, transparent, cloaked, equanimity, heartfelt, courageous, calm

Lessons: Loving Flow encourages us to be open and emotionally stable by looking at living vulnerably. What we think we hide, people can already see. Vulnerability feels wonderful. There is tremendous freedom in releasing internal pressures.

Practice: How have you protected yourself from vulnerability? Can you imagine what it would feel like to be open-hearted? Do you have examples in your life of anyone who lives with or has exhibited an open heart?

Next Step: Share honestly and authentically with everyone.

Contemplate: There comes a point in life when being vulnerable feels much better, and is easier, than holding on to our inner pains and insecurities.

Higher Octave: We can live in vulnerability, radiating to all and holding nothing back.

Affirmation: I am most beautiful when I am fully open.

RELEASING FLOW

Finding balance in relationships can be kind of rocky.
But that doesn't mean it isn't worth doing. Relationships shape us,
rubbing off our sharpest edges, smoothing out the highs and lows.
What a gift it is to be a friend, to have a friend, to know a friend.
That is how we can find true balance.

Experience: The Nature of Relationship

Our relationships with our mates, friends, family, co-workers, and neighbors are mirrors that reflect our own behaviors and attitudes. This is one of the most important ways that humans, as a social species, learn about ourselves and get the important feedback we need to make necessary evolutionary changes. Relationships don't have to look or be a certain way. At their core, they are all about relating.

When a relationship is working, the individuals share an ease with one another, have things in common, and offer differences that help each other grow. At their best, relationships of all kinds offer friendship, companionship, and sometimes partnership. We learn to support each other, giving and taking.

Relationships are also good vehicles for learning trust and feeling secure in the constant up and down wave-like action that exists in all human relations.

The Moon is 250,000 miles away and pulls on trillions of gallons of ocean water 24/7. Waves, ups and downs, and changes are natural to every aspect of earthly life. These changes offer opportunity for emotional and spiritual growth. We are supported in exploring our inner critics and personal challenges. We are encouraged to be our "real" *self* and thus to "peel the onion". We take a step by opening our hearts to love and our minds to the equality of others, living in compassion with a mindfulness towards the life that surrounds us.

Conversely, when relationships are at their worst, we exhibit sticky and needy behavior. We may call it love, but getting needs met is not unconditional love. Don't look to others to give you what you can give yourself. People can be attracted to us for "having it," but "wanting it" from others is not so attractive. Yes, we do this when we are young, but we do grow out of it.

When we have difficulty with other people, our difficulty may actually be with ourselves, not them. It may feel like they are pushing our buttons, but we learn to see that it is really about us having a button.

Relationships in our twenties usually contain a lot of unconscious behaviors. But this is how we learn and grow. At this age, we are not very objective in relationships. We mostly serve our ego's anxiety, sitting in a place of righteousness about how we act and what we deserve. Sometimes we even seek to change our mates into what we want without examining our own behaviors. A relationship centered on getting without giving may not last very long. And if it does, it's often unhealthy. When we want it all, we are not such good partners, friends, or family. Better to want to GIVE it all.

Are relationships necessary? Well, they don't seem to be. In fact, they can get in the way.

We can look to the inner guru and to life for the feedback we want. A relationship can get in the way when we are forced to live in constant compromises that feel unfair or unfulfilling. Why do some people not have good track records in relationships? Look to the level of honesty and selflessness as a clue. Why does one want that relationship? Is it about having convenience? Relationships will often come when we give up and stop looking.

Even in healthy relationships, it can be good to spend time apart. We need to be committed but we don't need to blend our whole lives. Spend some time apart and have a sense of individual identities. This is very important for some personality styles.

"Let there be spaces in your togetherness,
And let the winds of the heavens dance between you.

Love one another but make not a bond of love:
Let it rather be a moving sea between the shores of your souls."[1]

Let's relax, my friends. Dare to be intimate with another human being. Dare to be shown where you might be wrong. Connect with one another with honesty and sincerity. Don't be concerned about giving too much and keeping score on what you get. Sure, marriage and friendships are sometimes just a convenience, but we spend a very short time in these bodies. To be able to touch another human in a meaningful way is such an alive and transcendental experience. This is at the heart of the nature of relationship.

---

1   Gibran, Kahlil. *The Prophet. Alfred A. Knopf,* 1923.

Significance: The airy aspect of water, personal growth, rocky road, transformation, desires, attunement, empathy, selfishness, movement, changes, fulfillment, idealism, romance

Lessons: Releasing Flow shows us the way to be with others in our life. It can be unrewarding to live on an isolated island. The conscious one learns to see the other as *self.*

Practices: In what ways are your relationships important to you? Think about some lessons you have learned in your relationships. To have a friend, you need to be a friend. Do you believe this?

Next Step: Live with honesty, both with yourself and in your relation to others.

Contemplate: Does it give you more joy to give or to get?

Higher Octave: Relationships don't ever end, though they do transform.

Affirmation: I am equally open to all whom I meet.

OBSERVING FLOW

Life is a gift worth opening to and exploring fully. This gift is available each moment. It's waiting for us to be awake and ready. It doesn't have any strings attached, even if it's wrapped with a bow. It is just there. But it can expire. Opportunities can disappear. Being present sharpens the vision and helps us move into action when the time arises. Observing the flow in our life is a great initial step.

Experience: Use Your Gifts or Lose Them

On my thirtieth birthday, I was homesteading in Southern Oregon, living on eighty acres. We were living a natural lifestyle with organic gardens, food preservation, and outdoor living. Our first child was two that year, and it was a relaxed, quiet, rural life.

I had moved from New York City to San Francisco, then to the suburbs, and now to the rural countryside. It wasn't at all planned. It simply felt right to slow down enough to feel what was real and not real in order to let go of my conditioning; to enhance my coming into a sense of presence, and then to feel the next steps in life.

On that day of turning thirty, I got a very clear inward message—a cosmic kick in the pants: *if you don't use your gifts, you will lose the opportunity to use them over time.*

While we tend to focus our anguish on our challenges and bad habits, the truth is that these are balanced on some ethereal scale by qualities that can be seen as our gifts—our skills and abilities.

In adulthood, it is natural to work on our challenges. We meet them every day at work, in our relationships, and in our own areas of low self-esteem. So many books, magazines, and a myriad of media are designed to identify and support our improvements. As we age, decade by decade, we experience natural improvement. Progress and development come as we get clarity, and our attitudes change to improve our abilities in deficient areas.

Unlike our challenges, our gifts may not get as much attention. Sometimes, we even neglect them. It is easy to play piano, dance, or sing as a young child. Years later, if we get inspired to try them again, they may not be so easy. There is a window, as it were, for many of life's activities. Better kick up your heels, they say, before you get married and have kids. It's good to study a subject while in school because we might not have the same opportunity again later in life.

My gifts were doing business and being active in the outer community. That cosmic kick in the pants propelled me, seemingly directly, to open a vegetarian restaurant that was unique for the area and the time. This restaurant started a spiral of movements that has never really stopped. I never lived that quiet country life in the same way again, which is okay. After all, we get the gifts to use them, and for all things there is a season.

On a much deeper level, we, as beings, explore the questions of why we are here and what should we do? The idea of "purpose" is popular now. But I feel the question of purpose comes from the ego, and is driven by wanting to be seen. There is another sense of destiny, or perhaps fate, that is more cosmic-driven and less egoic. Destiny does not mean something will happen, but there is energetic motion in its direction. We have free will, so destiny may be a strong nudge, but not a *fait accompli.*

We feel that we are supposed to do certain things, but we put them off out of laziness and insecurity. We hesitate because we think we need more experience and wait for the proper moment to launch. We poll friends and family and check market forecasts. There is always a cloud on the horizon. We spend a lifetime paralyzed by fear, anger, or insecurity about what others think.

Would I have liked to have had this book published earlier in my life? Yes! But the truth is, I needed this amount of time and experience, plus my planetary energies, which are strong now, for it to be what it is. This is the time. Don't think that starting earlier means it will be finished earlier. So, my thirty-year-old self was realizing an important transitory point in life. We may not lose the gifts, but we do lose the opportunity.

My friends, these are dated offers because they, like all life, come and go. Your compulsion leaves you no choice but to move into activity at some point. Now is as good a time as any to get started. It only takes making one small (even baby) step in that direction. If we don't use our gifts for our life destinies, there will come a time when we will lose them.

Significance: The earthy aspect of water, destiny, future, freedom, expression, optimism, creativity, dreams, enthusiasm, undisciplined, rejection, insecurity, intuition

Lessons: Life is full of moments of creative opportunities that develop our intuitive and emotional nature. Observing Flow helps us to add our own discipline to an opportunity to achieve inspired results. While each opportunity is unique, many unique opportunities do present themselves in life.

Practices: In your heart of hearts, what would you like to do in this life, regardless of time, money, and ability? Is there something that someone you know owns or has accomplished that you admire? Embrace the idea of "dream and then do" flowing through your life.

Next Step: Quiet all the resistances that the mind generates over and over.

Contemplate: Trust your intuition; you are always on your path.

Higher Octave: See the Divine in all situations and moments.

Affirmation: The more I share with others, the more I love myself.

LIVING INTELLIGENCE

*Every day, we meet a symbolic fork in the road.
We can make a fresh choice about any area of our life at
any point in time. The forks may look like they are heading in
different directions, and they may end up in different places,
or meet up further down the road.*

Experience: Endgame

What is the goal or purpose of this life? Well, I'm not sure I want to touch that question right here. But surely we can agree that *living in peace and joy and getting out of suffering* as an endgame is a worthy substitute for an answer to this lofty question.

An endgame is the last stage of a game of chess or a process—the grand finale, the home stretch, the last/final straw, the last gasp. *The urban understanding of endgame is a relationship that appears to be unstoppable.* Sure, they just met, but they're endgame. They'll get married one day.

Aside from a romantic relationship, what is unstoppable for you?

The study of psychology—the science of mental life and behavior—has been mainstream and popular for nearly one hundred years. It provides important information for helping us better understand ourselves and our relationships. When we understand ourselves at a deeper level, we have more compassion toward others and our self.

Psychologists have intuited many ways to define and analyze our behavior by studying our response to stimuli. Theories abound about how and why we act the way we do. But the endgame in mundane psychology seems to be *observing behavior.* Psychology does not seem able to end our suffering.

Psychology has a newer transcendental side called transpersonal psychology that brings more depth and forward conclusions to these discussions. It extends psychology beyond the individual or personal viewpoint to our highest potential and transcendental states, thus integrating the spiritual and transcendent aspects of human experiences within the framework of modern psychology. Even within this depth, psychology has inherent constraints.

I have preferred to see life through the lens of spirituality. This is the root of my experiences for over fifty years.

Spirituality has an endgame of being in the moment. It can be experienced by clearing any triggers we have. When we are centered, nothing that touches us takes us out of this fullness. We need to get out of the reactions of the mind, quit our mental calisthenics, because we aren't able to experience peace there. True presence is not in the mind. It just exists; it can't be held.

We get triggered, and psychology can explain this very well, thus adding a dimension to the spiritual search. Spirituality encourages us to transcend the experiences of the trigger and come back to the moment or center. We don't need to understand the trigger. We don't need to agree with everything in our life. All we must do is accept what we can't accept. This is transcendence. It's an end to the game of games.

For some, going in circles and feeling the wind on our face may feel like enough. Krishna said that *out of a thousand seekers, only one truly knows me.* So, who will join in being that one as the endgame?

Significance: The fiery aspect of air, confidence, expression, flexibility, detached, level-headed, indecision, rationality, stubbornness, selfishness, wisdom, finding the way, determination

Lessons: Living Intelligence wants us to be our best. But when we choose unwisely, prejudice and malice can block our path. The wise ones see that no choice has to be made when we follow our heart.

Practices: What triggers you? How do you deal with being triggered? How does it feel to be in the moment?

Next Step: Stop trying to figure things out.

Contemplate: Conditions are always neutral. There is no "right" or "wrong" way to be.

Higher Octave: Free of thinking and the need to understand, we follow the path in front of us.

Affirmation: The quickest path home is one step at a time.

LOVING INTELLIGENCE

St. Francis of Assisi was a unique and mystical Italian saint who lived in the 1200s. St. Francis had a great love for animals and the environment. He gave that love and thanks to Brother Sun, Sister Moon, Brother Wind, Water, Fire, and Earth. When he preached to the birds, none flew away.

Experience: Codependence

At one point or another, most of us have claimed control over our life by exerting a righteousness about our independence, saying, "I don't need anyone or anything." There is a bit of arrogance in this statement. When we live this way, it may also include a dose of belligerence, unreasonableness, control, aggression, and a desire to dominate. The innate feeling may be to get away from neediness, but these attitudes are very needy— needy of being in control and needy of attention.

When I have clients with this type of attitude, I counter their mental and emotional contortions and bring a bit of perspective to their views. I say, "Have you ever eaten a banana?" They say, "Yes." I ask, "Do you have banana trees in your backyard?" "No." "Then you are dependent on someone else to grow, harvest, and truck those bananas to a local store." We don't refine our own gasoline, yet we use it to drive our cars. We haven't built our cars, and most of us don't service our cars, yet we have them at our disposal when we choose to use them.

Codependency in a relationship is when each person involved is mentally, emotionally, physically, and/or spiritually reliant on the other in a way that leads to dysfunctional patterns of behavior.

However, to some extent, we live in codependence with the rest of the world on pretty much every level. There would be no life, heat, or light anywhere in the solar system without the Sun. Without wind, rain, bees, and even cells, our human species would not exist. Everything works together for our betterment when we are able to live life with gratitude. The opposite of interdependence isn't codependence. Codependence still has some interdependence in it.

We are responsible for our part of this universal game. Responsibility can bring joy and meaning. Please don't get stuck in the burden of responsibility. Burdens appear when we have expectations and small sightedness. They come from taking ourselves too seriously. These burdens can cause stomach aches, headaches, and back pain. They make us rigid and inflexible.

Humans are a social species. We need the different skills and personalities of each person to make our societies work. What a dull world this would be if everyone thought just like me. But it takes far-sightedness to realize that by giving, we receive and by giving up our own opinions, we are rewarded with joy and freedom. The world is full of our brothers and sisters, and codependence on them can be joyful and freeing.

Prayer of St Francis

Lord, make me an instrument of your peace.
Where there is hatred, let me bring love.
Where there is offense, let me bring pardon.
Where there is discord, let me bring union.
Where there is error, let me bring truth.
Where there is doubt, let me bring faith.
Where there is despair, let me bring hope.
Where there is darkness, let me bring your light.
Where there is sadness, let me bring joy.
O Master, let me not seek as much
to be consoled as to console,
to be understood as to understand,
to be loved as to love,
for it is in giving that one receives,
it is in self-forgetting that one finds,
it is in pardoning that one is pardoned,
it is in dying that one is raised to eternal life.

Significance: the watery aspect of air, clarity, feelings, intelligence, growth, honesty, truth, narcissism, judgements, anxiety, not communicating, change, freedom, fresh perspectives

Lessons: Loving Intelligence wants to teach us that being resourceful is not the same as being independent. When our head rules over our heart, we make judgments that are not to be trusted. When we practice with native intelligence to follow our true feelings, we live in harmony with all life.

Practices: Can you name something that has no input or effect on anyone or anything? Appreciate the workers who are always there at our favorite stores and restaurants. Reflect on *Thy and I are one.*

Next Step: Start to recognize when you behave in old ways that don't serve you.

Contemplate: How much happier we are when we are in gratitude.

Higher Octave: Be true to the *self* .

Affirmation: I am one with all that I meet.

RELEASING INTELLIGENCE

Life can offer many perspectives, but none of them necessarily has a better outcome than another. The grass isn't always greener, just a different shade of green. Living this way takes practice. It helps to become surrendered, to love what we have, and to feel total and whole each moment.

Experience: The Better Story is No Story

Forty years ago, I remember reading a survey in the USA Today newspaper. They asked people from a cross section of economic levels, from rich to poor, if they were happy with their level of income. All of the respondents, regardless of their income level, responded that they wanted to make 10 percent more. Everybody wanted the same increase.

These days, 10 percent more isn't enough. The advertising industry is merciless about the implication that without the newest and best things, our life is incomplete. Without gusto, our life is bland. People are losers unless they have or do x, y, and z.

What I call data points—bits of information—have become an international obsession. How many confirming opinions do we need? How much stuff and how many accomplishments do we need?

The self-help community nowadays incessantly boosts the need to be better. Here are some typical samples of marketing email titles from my inbox:

Change Your Body, Change Your Brain.

Never Miss Another Important Event

Making Meaning of the Ending of Days

A "Party in the New Paradigm of Radical Love!"

The Superfoods That Saved Me

10 Best Yoga Poses to Become Taller

All of this is exhausting and impossible to keep up with. It creates overwhelm and confusion. Eli Jaxon-Bear is the first person I heard say that we can make our boxed-in prison as nice as we want it—80" color TV, sofas, mini bar, workout room, add all we want—but it's still a prison. The prison is your infected ideas, conditions, and limitations created by the unnecessary noise that gets absorbed into and is believed by our minds.

So, I came up with the best "better" story: no story. Be content with what we have. Live in the moment. Deal with the triggers as they come up, because as soon as we are triggered, our thinking, feeling, and doing are distorted.

We cannot see clearly once we are triggered because we are not in this moment. The story of no story is: I am that I am.

Otherwise, the wanting more never, ever ends. We must choose to change the game we play to no game at all. The new class, the new workout, the next date, the new restaurant, the next country, the next post—it'll never be enough to satisfy us.

There is freedom from the burden of needing anything because we already have all we need. New stuff still comes—we don't live in a black hole after all—and we can enjoy what comes without the questions of "When?" or "How?"

What do I do with my fixation? Fix it. See through it. Love it and the *self*. Read the books we have. Listen to all our records again. Appreciate those around us and all the experiences we enjoy. This may take a while, but it gives us something worthwhile to do with life while we realize that the better story is no story.

Significance: The earthy aspect of air, action, curiosity, commonsense, courage, truth, adaptability, questioning, fickleness, rebelliousness, vision, strength, assurance, quick thinking

Lessons: Releasing Intelligence appreciates that we are mentally capable and want to grow spiritually. When we move fast and hold on, we miss the subtleties of life. Being smart enough to trust intuition and attunement to details is a good long-term strategy.

Practices: Would you enjoy leading a simpler life? Are there stresses in your life that you can release? Do you buy into the media's messages?

Next Step: Slow down to speed up.

Contemplate: We can't figure out everything in life.

Higher Octave: Letting go of ideas enables more ideas to come.

Affirmation: All challenges help me to get closer to my goals.

OBSERVING INTELLIGENCE

*Words have great power and come with
intentional and unintentional meanings.
There is energy behind all our words.
Sometimes it's not what we say, but how we say it.*

Experience: The Power of Words

I had a Facebook friend write me recently in part, "We must abide..." I wrote him back, "Abide, not 'must' abide." "Abide," here, means a place to reside. The place we were talking about is enlightenment. He wrote back that he had a thing about "must", meaning he appreciated more awareness of his making pronouncements. "Must" means necessary, but do we know that something is really necessary? When we include "must" in our language, it changes the energy of our words, and many times, the thing we "must" doesn't happen. This type of language is limiting instead of expanding because it inherently implies lack.

There are groups of words and phrases we use and overuse in today's be-all society that are very sticky by nature. I don't think people realize the kind of power and difficulty created by these words.

Superlatives represent exaggerated expressions, and in general, the accuracy of expression is not highly valued by our society. It is easy to use and overuse superlatives because we are built on a superlative foundation. Best, greatest, largest, worst; we've become a world of Guinness World Records.

We don't really know what is the best or worst. Everything just is. The energy of comparisons takes us out of our center. Comparisons scream out to people. Some shout back, "You're wrong." Others shrink into the shell they've created to hide from being compared.

Words like "never," "always," and "most" get used indiscriminately without concern for their effect. Absolutes are anything but absolute. We can use "always" and "never" in the same breath. Are we trying to impress people? Are we needing to become an authority? Are we feeling a "never" in our life, so we feel the need to say "always"?

Emphatics and hyperbole scream LOOK AT ME. Is that what we want to say? Maybe it is. This is anxiety inducing. It isn't peaceful or balanced.

We use conditional statements like, "If you don't, then I won't" when we should be saying, "I wish you would." Don't make your actions depend on outside conditions. That sets the situation up for failure.

Master Yoda said, "Do or don't do. There is no try."

"I will try" doesn't really tell us anything. Is this what we want from people in our life? How does it feel coming at us? I consciously do not use this word because I know the inherent limitations in it.

When we change, "What I did" to "What got done," we don't break our arms patting ourselves on the back.

I have to say it again. These kinds of words and grammatical inferences are sticky. They can be a cause of disease and headaches. There is no way out of these energies unless we back off and relax. Most of these words are used unconsciously without any awareness of the potential fallout.

I prefer "unlikely" or "most likely". Doesn't that feel better? I like "please" with feelings of gratitude. "I wish." "Would you?" "Could you?" "I appreciate!" There is just as much power in these words and phrases, but with balance and peace.

Let's tune in to what we say and how we say it. Become more conscious of your energy, one phrase at a time. Focus on the power of your words!

Significance: The airy aspect of air, intellectual, direct, ungrounded, forceful, assertive, pushy, overbearing, intuition, understanding, sacrifice, awareness, limitation

Lessons: Observing Intelligence wants us to be aware of the limitations that bind us. Realize that these opportunities are gifts for our personal growth. We want to be able to express ourselves in ways others will hear and understand.

Practices: Notice the actual language that you and those around you use. What deeper meaning and energy do you feel when you use these kinds of words? Practice developing consciousness in your use of vocabulary. See if you can use softer phrases each day.

Next Step: Listen to yourself speak.

Contemplate: Mean what you say and say what you mean.

Higher Octave: When we stop self-sabotaging, we have no limits.

Affirmation: I follow the heart, not the head.

LIVING GRAVITY

Bananas and humans have more than 60 percent of the same DNA and are both in a constant state of ripening. Apparently, bananas enjoy the presence of other fruits and, when in close proximity, will help them to ripen. Humans are a social species. Much of our internal work is reflected by our connection to and response from others.

In his book, Life Changing Foods, Anthony Williams says, "Bananas strengthen the core of who we are, encouraging us to peel back our false shields, and expose our true selves. They can help reverse a state of mind that's saturated with fear (eating three or more a day can help reduce PTSD), and they help us express our true desire to be productive, overcoming procrastination and other unproductive behaviors in the process. If you think a friend is holding on to resentments, offer her or him a banana, and it will help dissolve the feelings of ill will." [1]

---

1   Williams, Anthony. *Medical Medium: Life Changing Foods. Save Yourself and the Ones You Love with the Hidden Healing Powers of Fruits & Vegetables. Hay House, LLC,* 2016.

Experience: An Ap-pealing Story

In this fast-paced, modern world, those of us with spiritual goals tend to want results NOW. Counter-intuitively, when our thoughts and actions are focused on continuous wanting, we push our highest potential away instead of drawing it closer.

A few weeks ago, while making breakfast, I was struck by the wisdom of the humble banana and its gradual ripening process. In our "green" form, humans have many unripe goals and desires. This is a big development because we have spent a long time not knowing what we want. This stage can be frustrating because we see other humans riper than us, and we want more. We can spend our life wanting to be somewhere we are not. Can we end that story?

There is a teaching story from India that I first heard many decades ago. This is the kind of story that has been told for millennia and has been shared in many different versions.

An old Indian guru master is sitting alone with a few of his most senior disciples in a quiet place in the ashram. One disciple asks the guru,

"Master, when will I wake up?"

"This lifetime, beloved," The Master shares in response.

"Oh, thank you, Master!!!"

The one sitting next to this disciple feels emboldened and says to the Master, "Oh Master, when will *I* wake up?"

The Master gently answers this student, "Next lifetime!"

"Oh, thank you, Master," he says, inwardly glowing at this promise.

A third disciple also asks, "Master, when will I awake?"

"In two lifetimes, my son," says the Master.

The disciple replies, "Thank you, Master."

Now, the greatest disciple of them all, Sage Narada, feels it is his time to make the same inquiry of the Master. "Master, when will I wake up?" he asks.

The Master answers, "Narada, in one million lifetimes!"

Narada, in reply, says, "Thank you, Master."

The Master then gets up to leave the room, and at the same time, Narada gets up to go outside. The remaining disciples look at each other in amazement. How could the greatest of them all need one million lifetimes? "Poor Narada," they mutter to themselves. At this point, they notice that Narada is dancing outside.

The disciples go outside to see how Narada is doing. One says to him, "Did you not hear what Master said to you, Narada?"

"Yes, I heard," he says.

"It will take one million lives for you to wake up," the disciple says, trying to convey disappointment.

Narada stopped his joyous dancing and said to his brother disciple, "Did you not hear what he said, brother? Be in my joy with me. He said I will wake up." At that moment, he wakes up.

This is the test of our ripening. To feel joy in the journey and not have our eyes on some possible future date or achievement. Our wanting in life keeps us wanting. Like the banana, we *will* ripen and become an ap-pealing story.

Significance: The fiery aspect of earth, success, practical, earthy, maturity, materialism, stubborn, impractical, reap, pragmatic, lazy, disorganized, generous, secure, abundance

Lessons: Living Gravity knows that through hard focused work we can meet all goals. When we become stubborn and small-minded, our emotional and spiritual needs are not met. Living with a positive attitude brings wealth and success in all ways.

Practices: Can you see how you have changed and grown over the years? Do you have the patience to wait for the things you want in life? Notice the patience level of people around you.

Next Step: Strive to develop clarity about what is important to you in this life.

Contemplate: In this moment, everything is perfect as it is.

Higher Octave: Things come on their own when the moment is right.

Affirmation: As diamonds are made from charcoal, so can I evolve.

LOVING GRAVITY

The original 19th-century story of Goldilocks was written about an old woman and three bachelors. While long ago, the tale was interpreted as a metaphor for the hazards of wandering off and exploring strangers' houses, it is typically framed today as a discovery of what is "just right." The story shows us the importance of the middle path between opposites. This concept spread across many different disciplines like psychology, biology, and astronomy, where it is called the Goldilocks Principle. For example, a planet that is neither too cold nor too hot while orbiting its sun is just the right distance to foster biological life and is said to be in the Goldilocks Zone.

Experience: The Middle Path of Moderation

I want to share one of life's lessons that I learned a long time ago.

I'm an enthusiastic native New Yorker and an extrovert by nature. My whole life, I needed to learn to rein in my energy. It became an early lesson to live in the center.

What is the center? The center is neither too much nor too little; not excessive and not small. The center is, like in pottery on the wheel, perfectly round, with nothing sticking out. It is a place of least resistance. Spiritually, the center is the heart of any teaching that is reached by keeping our needs, expectations, and attitudes minimized because they send us off our center. How do we get there? By living the middle path of moderation.

There is another story of the middle path— one close to my heart. Buddha was in his ascetic stage when he became so emaciated that his bones were showing through his skin. He was living asceticism in an extreme. Then a local village girl named Sujata offered him milk and rice pudding. Realizing the importance of The Middle Way— a path of moderation, away from the extremes of self-indulgence—Buddha regained his strength and soon found Enlightenment under the nearby Bodhi Tree.

People starting on a diet or exercise routine tend to burn themselves out in the first few days because they alter their routine too significantly. This is human nature. It's easy to go from one extreme to another, missing the center along the way. When ending a prolonged fast, we need to return to regular eating carefully. If we start too quickly, we can hurt ourselves a bit, in addition to losing the value gained by the fast.

Sometimes we need to find center by increasing our output. Other times, through reduction. The middle path requires balance in the center of all the alternatives. Walking a tightrope or on a narrow ledge, the body finds a way to compensate, making micro adjustments in order to stay balanced. This happens in tree pose in yoga. We put our hands out to the sides to balance the energy. Somehow, we naturally know the right way.

My secret to finding balance was to move over a little on to the path of moderation in any situation. Changing too much, too frequently, is an emotional reaction and will take us to the other extreme. Moving a little bit is a better approach when centering. Small steps can lead to large gains.

The middle path and moderation may not seem full of sizzle. It certainly isn't the stuff that headlines are made of. And yet, it has so much to offer. We can feel unseen internal gains that we can feel when going about our life in a moderate way. Moderation leaves energy to do more; extremes tire us out. Moderation doesn't have much drama. For any goal or challenge, I suggest a moderate approach. I think over time, you'll find the middle path of moderation has plenty of sizzle.

Significance: The watery aspect of earth, gentle, calm, growth, fruitful, introverted, cautious, wise, insecure, selfish, self-care, truth, grounded, stoic, vision, stability in a moving world

Lessons: Loving Gravity reminds us that living without gratitude is like living in a desert. The simple things in life offer depth beyond any modest exterior. Being present, no matter the place or moment, makes everything we attempt successful.

Practices: In what ways do you live in extremes? Do you know anyone in your life who embodies a sense of moderation? Reflect on the ways in which you do live or do not live from your center.

Next Step: Notice when you act from extremes.

Contemplate: Why do I not take better care of this body?

Higher Octave: Simple acts have magical qualities.

Affirmation: I care for and love this earth and everything here, including myself.

RELEASING GRAVITY

Coconuts were used as a form of currency in some ancient societies. They were particularly valuable in island cultures where they were an important source of food and other resources. In India, they are considered the most sattvic fruit and, thus, the purest fruit one can offer to God. There is a nobility to coconuts with their tough outer shell and sweet, delicate insides. They are associated with fertility, prosperity, and good fortune.

Experience: Money

We put a lot of our life energy into thinking about, attaining, or keeping money. Money may not be the root of all evil, but it sure does tie up a lot of energy, and not always in a healthy way.

Factually, we do need money to live. We have necessities, and exchanging money for them is efficient. However, problems arise when we tie up power and ego into money because then it can start to have bigger, stickier meanings. Or, we deflate ourselves over not having money and slip into feelings of unworthiness.

As Releasing Intelligence referenced, years ago, there was a survey question about how the respondents felt concerning the amount of money they had. Everyone, no matter their level of financial security, answered that they wanted about 10 percent more.

Without trying to make anything right or wrong, I want to share something about money to help clarify the ideas that often surround it. Societies, collectively, hold different ideas about money. To some, it is very important. Others, while still needing it, do not make it a central focus. They get by in ways that are efficient and dignified. I say dignified because we know people who do the opposite—who make sure that everyone around them knows that they have money, or want money, or are concerned about money. There is a lot of "money" in that sentence. That is the feeling we get around them.

These dynamics are complicated by the fact that a lot of the ideas we have about money are transferred to us by conditioning and imprinting by parents and society. The ideas we hold may not even be ours. Many parents, through no fault of their own, live with an expectation that their children should work to accomplish and attain everything they could not.

As sensitive children, we pick up on this expectation and live with it unconsciously. We may pursue a career that doesn't really satisfy us. We can do this for a long time, the same way we often stay in bad relationships. But in our seeking, we can eventually come to a place of understanding who we are and what we want. Finally, we can come into our own identity.

"Worthwhile" may not have anything to do with money. What an interesting word worthwhile is. Worth our while; to have a value equivalent to the time and effort engaged. Mustn't we judge that for ourselves? No one else can make that determination for us.

I'm thinking of a common example of a young person who wants to pursue art as a career, but is deterred by parents or teachers who tell them they can't support themselves with art. Though thinking in terms of financial gain might be realistic, what's equally realistic is the joy that comes from doing something one feels called to do. Thank goodness many of these types of familial battles have been fought in the past so that younger generations might be freer to choose careers based on their own joy instead of financial potential.

Money is a way to be heard. We can think of money in a very paternalistic way in terms of control and power. But we can also balance this out with the many positive possibilities money can provide, like getting an education or going on a trip. We can give money away to others who need it. We can buy ways to communicate with money, like art supplies or social media ads. Having a computer is a tool we can use to write a book like this one. Let's use our money for creation and in creative ways.

Living life, following karma, and doing duty may not be centered around money. Money may not come into play at all. Clients ask me what they should do when they have questions about their careers. I tell them, "You know what you want to do." They say, "You mean THAT?" I say, "Yes." People know in their hearts what they want to do. In life, we can learn to release whatever is holding us back from doing what we really want to do.

Let's see money as the natural form of energy it is, not some God that we put on a pedestal. Is life easier with money? Absolutely! Does it bring happiness? No, not really. Happiness needs to be there on its own. Money is a means, not an end. With that in mind, it is best to keep an eye on your true goal in life.

Do what you love and the money will follow. I know it is a little cliché, but there is truth to this idea, isn't there? This is a healthy way to live, oriented not so much around results, but the journey to the results. The necessity of money does force us to make decisions and move in certain directions. It can be extremely painful, but in the end, we are better for the challenges. We must appreciate what we have; we must appreciate life as it is. When we see money as neutral and take on our challenges with a wholesome spirit, more doors open. The necessity for money ends up pushing us into our truth. That lesson is something that money can't buy.

Significance: The airy aspect of earth, hardworking, fair, wisdom, reliable, stable, scheming, greedy, irresponsible, envious, jealous, good planner, patience, perseverance, common sense

Lessons: Releasing Gravity shows us that efficiency in effort can pay off in physical success. When we push our way forward, we may not always like the result. Always keep at least one eye on the journey, not on the destination.

Practices: How is your energy around money? How do you feel about people around you who have money? Let's find a balance with the money in our life. Honor what you have and keep it moving for others.

Next Step: Take an inward survey. Are you happy with the directions your life is going?

Contemplate: Only I can give me what I long for.

Higher Octave: The best things in life are free.

Affirmation: I will focus all my energy on moving in the same direction.

OBSERVING GRAVITY

Many experiences make up a lifetime. One time I took a bus in India. I arrived an hour early at the bus stand. They immediately directed me over to a bus and told me to get on board. I found out that this bus was supposed to leave an hour earlier, but was seemingly sitting and waiting for me. Talk about just in time! I learned this because a friend of mine—someone with whom I was hoping to connect—was on the bus. We had a lovely time on our journey.

Experience: Life is a Long Journey

One of life's ironies is that most of us don't live in the moment—this free moment of no past or future, of connection to all life in which nothing is perceived as missing. It's this moment that humanity longs for, even if humanity doesn't consciously know it exists.

We have all lived in moments of being stuck, thinking that the way life is now is how it will always be. For example, depression is a feeling of helplessness where we perceive our circumstances to be unhappy, bleak, and unchanging. We forget the better times of the past and fail to see the possibility of upward ticks ahead. When depressed, we sink into moments that are not connected to friends and family, and have trouble climbing out of the hole we dig.

Even in less dire situations, we can feel stuck at a dead end:

I'm single now and I'll never get married. Who would want me?

I'll never be able to get a good job and will be stuck at this terrible one forever.

My health condition will never change. The doctors don't know what to do with me.

Another irony is that by affirming these life conditions, we make it harder to get out of them. We close the curtains and wonder why there is no sunlight inside the room. We eat a diet we know is not right and wonder why the body reacts. We hate our job and wonder why we feel negative vibes from the boss. Silly us, stuck in that proverbial deep hole.

We need encouragement not to get stuck at a bus stop thinking this is all there is. All things change in this life. The Buddhists call this impermanence (16 The Tower). Everything changes. I find this to be a very uplifting sentiment because it releases a feeling of burden that I must be responsible for every change and every plan. The leaves fall off the trees in autumn without my doing anything. The birds migrate without participation. These are easy to see.

To everything, there is a season. The joy in life we learn, is not so much getting to a destination, as much as enjoying the stops along the way. The hard times have value. I hope you never forget that. Appreciate the freedom of the single life. Enjoy the kids while they are young. Get clear about what does motivate you and what you want to do in your life. Take responsibility for your body's health. I am convinced there is a body/mind connection. The pills often don't work because we keep reinfecting ourselves.

Come to live fully engaged in every present moment, not sunk into a pit. Our bus stops are necessary and even helpful. We feel a level of joy when we stop hiccupping. I appreciate when I stop banging my toes. So too are the dips and maybe even the depressions, to be seen as great friends. Life is a long journey.

Significance: The earthy aspect of earth, youthful, opportunity, fresh, eager, renewal, selfish, rebellious, bounty, creativity, learning, self-pity, judgmental, grounded, assurance

Lessons: Observing Gravity sees that we are not always at the beginning steps, even if it may feel that way. Life is evolving through us each moment. Each experience is new, but our sensitivity to experience is expanding to meet them.

Practices: Have you ever looked back on a terrible situation as a blessing in disguise? Can you see value in difficult experiences? Reflect on the nature of situations in your life during which you might have felt an inclination to blame others.

Next Step: Look at any burdens you may carry with you.

Contemplate: I am changing each day.

Higher Octave: Go with the flow.

Affirmation: I'm awake and ready!

THE MINOR TRUTHS

ACE of ENERGY

Mahavatar Babaji has resided for hundreds, perhaps thousands, of years in a remote Himalayan region of India, seen in person by only a small number of disciples and others. He is reputed to be ageless. Paramahansa Yogananda reported that Babaji's age, family, place of birth, true name, and other details about his life are unknown. He did write that Babaji has a sister called Mataji (meaning "Holy Mother") who has also lived throughout the centuries. Her level of spiritual attainment is comparable to her brother's, and she lives in a state of spiritual ecstasy in a cave.

Experience: Babaji

Sometimes the great ones, in many areas of life, are known by the simplest of names. For instance, there are many teachers known as *Maharaji* in India. *Maharaji* translates to "great king." *Sufi* is a generic term meaning "man in wool." *Babaji*, in many languages, simply means "father". The *ji* at the end of the word is a term of endearment, changing the meaning to "revered father".

While Babaji can be a common name in India, there is one Babaji that stands out above all others. I have been aware of him for a very long time and I want to introduce him to you.

This Babaji was first announced to the world in Paramahansa Yogananda's classic spiritual book, *Autobiography of a Yogi*, written in 1946. Much of the knowledge we have of this particular Babaji is from this book. What I am about to share may seem unbelievable. But when we live closer to Divinity and in possibilities, we feel that all things are possible.

Babaji is said to be a deathless Mahavatar and is the head of the spiritual lineage to which Yogananda belonged. *Avatar* means "descent of a deity" in Sanskrit and *maha* means "great".

Sri Yukteswar, Yogananda's guru, explained to Yogananda that, "Babaji's spiritual state is beyond human comprehension... the dwarfed vision of men cannot pierce to his transcendental star. One attempts in vain even to picture the avatar's attainment. It is inconceivable."[1]

Yogananda says that Babaji and Jesus got together long ago and split up the world. Babaji is in charge of the Eastern part. He explains:

"The *Mahavatar* is in constant communion with Christ; together they send out vibrations of redemption and have planned the spiritual technique of salvation for this age. The work of these two fully-illuminated masters—one with the body, and one without it—is to inspire the nations to forsake suicidal wars, race hatreds, religious sectarianism, and the boomerang-evils of materialism. Babaji is well aware of the trend of modern times, especially of the influence and complexities of Western civilization, and realizes the necessity of spreading the self-liberations of yoga equally in the West and in the East."[2]

Lahiri Mahasaya, a disciple of Babaji, said, "Whenever anyone utters with reverence the name of Babaji, that devotee attracts an instant spiritual blessing."[3]

There are two stories of Babaji described in *Autobiography of a Yogi* that give us some insight into the nature of this Divine being. They were relayed by one of Yogananda's

---

1   Yogananda, Paramahansa. *Autobiography of a Yogi. Crystal Clarity Publishers*, 1946. p. 290.
2   Yogananda, Paramahansa. *Autobiography of a Yogi. Crystal Clarity Publishers*, 1946. p. 291-293.
3   Yogananda, Paramahansa. *Autobiography of a Yogi. Crystal Clarity Publishers*, 1946. p. 293.

teachers, who was able to join Babaji for a time.

Babaji has lived in the Himalayas for a long time. He travels with a small band of disciples, sometimes by walking from peak to peak and sometimes by instantaneously disappearing and reappearing in another place.

One time, this teacher relates, the band was sitting around a campfire for a Vedic ceremony when Babaji picked up a burning log and struck one of the men, burning his bare shoulder. The crowd was stunned, gasping at what the great master had done. Babaji explained that this man's karma was to die in a blaze, consumed by fire. By lightly striking his arm, he had mitigated that karma. Babaji then put his Divine hands on the man's burn and healed it.

Another story from the book is otherworldly.[4] Atop a mountain peak, Babaji and his disciples were startled by the appearance of a man who had climbed to the top looking for Babaji. After months of relentless searching, the man announced his desire to be accepted by Babaji as a disciple. Babaji was unmoved by the man's passionate plea. The man reacted by stating that his life was not worth living without the great master and that he would jump from the mountain peak if not accepted. Babaji's response was, "Jump then, I cannot accept you in your present state of development." The man then threw himself off the mountain peak, falling thousands of feet to his death.

Babaji instructed his shocked disciples to go down and retrieve the man's body. They carried the body back up to the peak and placed the body at the feet of their master. Babaji put his healing hand on the man's mangled body, and to everyone's surprise, the man woke up and bowed at Babaji's feet. Babaji said to him, "You are now ready for discipleship." Babaji beamed lovingly on his resurrected chela (disciple). "You have courageously passed a difficult test. Death shall not touch you again; now you are one of our immortal flock."

I've been inspired by Babaji's existence and these stories for decades.

In the last years, as the pace of life quickens and the stakes of existence seemingly become larger, we are naturally opened to deeper possibilities in our life. These possibilities, though a great gift, do not come without personal challenges and doubt. Wanting to become "bigger" is a big step, but becoming bigger is an even greater step.

Recently, I had occasion to connect with Babaji's presence. I received some spiritual guidance, healing, and support for the very project you hold in your hands. In writing this book, I experienced an inward wisdom about the importance of each and every one of my thoughts and actions. I deepened again on the infinite possibilities that await us. I was humbled by my own subtle ignorance and arrogance. I was inspired by the role you and I—we—can play in appreciating each atom and electron that comprises our life. I am in awe of having vehicles (book and body) to share my version of good news without any

4   Yogananda, Paramahansa. *Autobiography of a Yogi. Crystal Clarity Publishers*, 1946. p. 295.

desire for benefit in return.

In doubting moments—when you feel a hole in your life, or a need to avoid or be right, or pride is holding you back—please remember these words, "Whenever anyone utters with reverence the name of Babaji, that devotee attracts an instant spiritual blessing."

Significance: Fire, strong energy, transformation, desires, ambition, frustration, creation, support, enthusiasm, initiative, courage, selfish, demanding, unyielding, unconscious, new directions

Lessons: The Ace of Energy inspires us to remove all blocks and our limitations. Sometimes we have to be shaken to our core to break through to new energy levels and be aware of deeper consciousness. Find freedom in *knowing* and living the soul's destiny.

Practices: Can you believe and not believe? True or false: There is some depth in life you have not touched yet. Be like a fireman, ready for the call in each moment.

Next Step: To realize we are never alone or unsupported.

Contemplate: I am always loved and appreciated.

Higher Octave: What some call miracles are everyday occurrences to others.

Affirmation: I am strong, powerful, and able.

2 of ENERGY

I grew up in the 1950s, a time when modern stresses were just developing (though some voices already cried of ills). It was a different time. There was pressure of nuclear war and lots of social barriers, but it was slower paced and the hills we climbed didn't feel so high as they do now, nor were there as many of them. Unconscious behavior was common. Life wasn't "consciousness this" and "consciousness that" like it is now.

As we seemingly reach close to Doomsday Clock midnight—running with the briefcase in hand—we feel hurried, tense, and not in integrity. It's also hard to sleep, thanks to too much stimulus, demands, expectations, shame, and fears. The stress from world population growth (a fourfold increase in a century) has applied additional pressure in many ways.

Experience: Stresses of Modern Life

I was able to spend considerable time outside the United States for twenty years. This travel afforded many advantages, not the least of which is a broader perspective on life in the Western world, and the U.S. in particular. There is an adjustment when going to and from Asia. We—most travelers and I—can feel the palpable changes, even at the airports.

In Western society, the pace of life is faster—cars drive faster, people move faster. The amount of advertising is huge, not just on billboards, but subtle (or not so subtle) hits of information designed to influence us even when we aren't really interested. They attack our peace of mind if we let them. The sheer pace and intensity of life, the energy needed to be successful and secure basic needs, and the expectations we put on ourselves are overwhelming and not health-inducing.

Stress affects bodies and minds in many ways. Body chemistry is altered. Food does not digest as well, which, in turn, changes the functioning capacity in other bodily systems. Then the dominoes begin to fall. People get backaches and headaches. I see many people with stiff, painful bodies and rigid, painful thinking. Stress changes our personality. We adopt to other personas to compensate for life's challenges.

Some of us rely on doctors to heal stress-induced illness—which is really an epidemic in modern life. Doctors prescribe medicines and tell us to heal the condition. And though this may help to some extent, we infect ourselves again with unhealthy thinking and actions. Sometimes, simply thinking the solution won't work keeps it from working.

We have to be actively conscious to keep modern stress at bay. Meditation and yoga are helpful and very popular worldwide. Feeling gratitude and loving are an excellent diet. Honest communication and consciously releasing tensions can deflect the effects of stress. Invite prana into your body. Time alone in nature can be a very healthy and essential practice.

The ability to be in balance, receive guidance, and maintain realistic perspectives on our life situations can stimulate feelings of support. We don't want to sit in hopelessness. Having a bird's-eye view can mitigate some stress, especially when we get stuck in thinking things won't change. We can stop judging our thoughts and actions, and the actions of others. The more we appreciate ourselves for what we do, the better we feel. Modern life isn't getting any easier. We must find bold solutions to distance ourselves from the stresses of modern life.

Significance: Mars in Aries, fierceness, anger, balance, accomplishment, desires, disillusionment, patience, delays, unknown, centering, forward moving, planning, limitations

Lessons: The 2 of Energy says now is the time. But without focus and discipline, chaos may not become order. The wise one is prepared and ready, and can find the balance needed for success.

Practices: Think about the areas of your life where you feel stress. What solutions come to mind when you decide to prioritize reducing stress? Can you take on less, do less, and be happier?

Next Step: Slow down (or speed up, if necessary) and develop objectivity about any situation in your life.

Contemplate: A positive attitude helps bridge difficult times.

Higher Octave: I rise above all distractions.

Affirmation: I am master of my domain.

3 of ENERGY

Reflections help us see, but only when we are ready.
Acting as a mirror—being a reflection for someone else—is something
we can do for each other. When we are terrified of the lion within us,
we suppress our strengths; we doubt our abilities and gifts. Some of
our greatness is already there, and some needs to be developed.
It's a marathon, not a sprint. Even lions have ways they can grow,
like learning the value of saving a mouse who can pull a thorn from
the lion's paw.

Experience: The Lion Who Thought He Was a Sheep

There once was a lion that grew up in a flock of sheep. He didn't know he was a lion. He bleated and ate grass like a sheep. One day, the flock was wandering at the edge of a big jungle when a mighty lion let out a roar and leaped out of the forest right into the middle of the flock. All the sheep scattered away. Imagine the surprise of the jungle lion when he saw this other lion among the sheep. So, he gave chase. He got hold of him. The king of the jungle lion said to the cowering lion, "What are you doing here?"

The other lion said, "Have mercy on me. Don't eat me. Have mercy on me." But the king of the jungle dragged him away, saying, "Come with me." He took the lion to a lake and said, "Look." So, the lion who thought he was a sheep looked and saw his reflection for the first time. He saw his image. Then he looked at the jungle lion, looked in the water again, and let out a mighty roar. He was never a sheep again. It only took one minute.

I share this story here—one that I have used in many of my sessions—because all of us have a lion inside of us. If we don't see it, we live sheepishly.

We need to find the courage of our lion part and see through the sheepishness. The sheepishness is of our own making. Sure, we can blame events or other people for our actions. This is easy to do.

Harder, and more satisfying, is to look at ourselves with objectivity. If we can let go of the ideas of the mind, release a lifetime of doubt and fear, and be vulnerable and open to new ideas, we can see a new perspective—even if for just ONE second. We can feel like a new person—like a new Moon, or a sunrise—and become as we are and always have been to be what Divinity wishes for us and what our ancient relatives and angels are guiding us towards. When we come to and live from Truth, we are in the peaceful, quiet place of our highest potential. It's time to stop living like the lion who thought he was a sheep.

Significance: Sun in Aries, ability to move forward, clear vision, cooperation, see things as they are, self-confidence, anxiety, doubts, action, self-involvement, motion, initiative

Lessons: The 3 of Energy shares that we already have what we need to be who we want to be. We just need to be able to see it in ourselves. When we live in balance, we know we have all we will ever need.

Practices: What do you see when you look in the mirror? Ask others what they see when they look at you. Have you grown out of any sheepish behavior?

Next Step: Be honest with yourself about your integrity.

Contemplate: To live in *truth* is to know Truth.

Higher Octave: I see that I'm the one holding me back.

Affirmation: The small self doesn't serve me.

4 of ENERGY

Like fireworks illuminating the night sky above a golden temple catches our attention, a guru provides light and wisdom that help us look honestly at life and ourselves.

Experience: The Value of a Guru

At some point, individuals on the spiritual path will explore whether or not they need a guru. I want to examine this question in a way that values the way teachers play roles in all of our lives.

When I say guru, I mean the traditional Indian version of a guru. However, the term guru can also refer to many other kinds of teachers and mentors in a variety of roles.

In Sanskrit, *guru* means "the one who dispels the darkness and takes us towards light." *Gu* means darkness and *ru* means dispeller. Being in the light with a guru can spark awakening. Simply living in the moment and becoming aware of our own patterns can spark awakening too.

Any teacher can teach us. If we're open to it, every person we meet in life is a teacher.

The light and wisdom our teachers offer help us grow in every phase of our life.

Here are some common characteristics of a guru. These can also be applied to any teacher.

1. Gurus help us learn to observe our behavior. They support our living in the moment. They teach us about navigating our life. We have to do the work ourselves, but they show us the path and guide us along the way.

2. They help us develop our intuition and sensitivity. This may come from things they don't say, but convey silently. It may come from expressions of their intuition. Then, we learn how to clone their energy through magnetism. In essence, we develop our intuition by being near them.

3. Gurus demonstrate how to behave. This covers the little things in life—politeness in social situations, how to treat people who are rude or misbehaving, and sensitivity when it's called for in serious situations. We learn this from the rules of their organization, or, sometimes, from a lack of rules.

The Sanskrit word *bhava* applies here. At its most basic, it means "habitual or emotional tendencies," but I learned it as more about our vibration in a situation, or a place's vibration. The slang term "vibe" is very similar. Bhava becomes a way to act or be—an energy that is given off. A guru will teach this by how they are, not what they say.

4. A guru may be surrounded by a *sangha,* or community—the brothers and sisters (*gurubais*) in the group learning from the guru. This group offers an opportunity to receive feedback on our progress on the path. Noticing where we rub each other with irritation is a great teacher. We also have opportunities for *seva* service, by doing little projects to

maintain the group or take care of the sangha's shared space. Taking care of the guru's needs creates a wonderful spirit and conveys the teachings in practical ways.

5. Last, but not least, is the transmission. Whether this is through an initiation, *shakti*, grace, or channeling, a spirit wordlessly comes through the gurus. It is what gives the guru their power—not the knowledge, experience, or look, but something more instinctive or basic in their energy. It's an aura or vibration that makes them bigger than life. For a guru, this comes from their lineage and the spiritual family from which they descended.

No matter whether we're talking about a yoga teacher, a minister in a local church, or a knowledgeable, supportive coworker, many of these qualities are still relevant. These teachers share with us what they know. Sometimes, after a while, we learn to know what they are going to say next. We start to act like them, sometimes wearing similar outfits or colors of clothing. We might even start to have similar interests. A yoga class, church congregation, or group of co-workers acts as the *sangha*. Any teacher has teachers from whom they've learned. In some cases, those teachers give them the power to do what they do. The reverence we feel about them (the ones that came before) is the transmission.

Finding a guru can be like dating. At a young age, we meet people and we fool around, but we aren't ready to commit to a relationship for the rest of our life. Finding one to marry is like choosing a guru. There comes a moment, sometimes when we least expect it, when we meet someone and our heart just knows. There is no doubt because the heart is open. It's not something you choose, it's something that chooses you. It's a path you have to follow.

These kinds of relationships are valuable because they encourage us to live beyond our perceptions and needs. We can get isolated in daily life and forget to live from a bigger picture, beyond a self-centered orientation. Working with teachers offers inward growth and an opportunity for change. The egotistical self is always stretched in the process.

A life of eighty or so years has many hills and valleys. Some have lived their whole life in one house. Others trace time through many cycles. The guru/teacher experience is an important cycle in anyone's life. This changes as we develop satisfaction from within, which seems like a natural progression to me. The higher *self* becomes the guru to the self, like when we meet a newborn baby, and in this baby's innocence and emptiness, we learn again the value of a guru.

Significance: Venus in Aries, stability, harmony, family, unity, resolution, acceptance, equanimity, judgments, comparisons, jealousy, contemplation, completion

Lessons: The 4 of Energy wants our dreams to come true. All past contradictions and oppositions have to come to peace. When the student is ready, the guru appears.

Practices: Explore what you have learned from a guru/teacher you had in the past. Have you ever disagreed with a guru/teacher? Can you be objective about the cause of your reaction at the time? What would you like to learn from a guru/teacher?

Next Step: Take a deep breath. Allow the love inherent in the breath to fill your heart.

Contemplate: I celebrate what life gives me.

Higher Octave: Peace and love are their own reward.

Affirmation: I am ready to be my best self.

5 of ENERGY

Sometimes we wait for the rain to end, hoping for a rainbow to appear. Whether it's rain or reign, when we sit in unhappiness that we create, the solution is the same: Know that the rainbow is waiting for us.

Experience: The Reign of Errors

I've been running into this a lot lately with clients. Like a mouse chasing its tail, people get stuck in their own tight circles. Their perceived limitations become a self-fulfilling prophecy. All personalities can do this, which is why it's good to be aware of the mind/body connection. Our thoughts affect our body and what happens to us.

According to Wikipedia, a self-fulfilling prophecy is "a prediction that directly or indirectly causes itself to become true, by the very terms of the prophecy itself, due to positive feedback between belief and behavior."

Although examples of such prophecies can be found in literature as far back as ancient Greece and ancient India, it is 20th-century sociologist Robert K. Merton who is credited with coining the expression "self-fulfilling prophecy" and formalizing its structure and consequences. In his 1948 article, "Self-Fulfilling Prophecy," Merton defines it in the following terms:

> "The self-fulfilling prophecy is, in the beginning, a false definition of the situation evoking a new behavior which makes the original false conception come true. This specious validity of the self-fulfilling prophecy perpetuates a reign of error. For the prophet will cite the actual course of events as proof that he was right from the very beginning. In other words, a positive or negative prophecy, strongly held belief, or delusion—declared as truth when it is actually false—may sufficiently influence people so that their reactions ultimately fulfill the once-false prophecy."

This is sticky behavior, and part of a swift neurological cascade that follows a triggering thought or experience. You think he won't call, and then he doesn't. You think the car won't start, and then it doesn't. Say enough times that you are not good enough and people around you will start believing you. A potential job opportunity says they will call in the morning. It's now a few minutes after noon, and the mind starts down a trail: *I won't get the job, then I won't have a place to live, then I'll lose all my friends, and I'll never eat again. I'm going to die on a park bench within a week because no one will stop to help me because I'm such a loser.* Our mental suffering continues, without even noticing it until the company calls at 2:00 PM to say, "Sorry, I didn't call you in the morning."

It may take living through our twenties and thirties to break these patterns of thought. It may take longer. Learning to notice when it happens will help a lot. To end our suffering from mental ideas, we learn to assume our own self-worth and the possibilities surrounding us. We need to learn the difference between realism and fantasy. Take deep breaths and ask yourself, *Do I know whether what I'm thinking is true*? This alone can help us stop living in a self-induced reign of errors.

Significance: Saturn in Leo, difficulties, strife, competition, change, disruption, reorganization, cooperation, fear, bitterness, focus, overwhelm, small steps, blockage

Lessons: The 5 of Energy wants to clear the air and help us prepare for what lies ahead. Clearing the air helps us see that changes need to come from within. Saturn shows us that a focused, step-by-step approach is the most direct way.

Practices: Can you think of a time in your own life when you created a self-fulfilling prophecy? Can you trace the trail of negative reactions that came from it? What would happen if, instead of only focusing on fearful outcomes, you saw all the possibilities in any situation?

Next Step: Notice when a cascading mental story is running in your mind.

Contemplate: Stop wasting energy on erroneous ideas and fantasies.

Higher Octave: I am not responsible for events outside of me.

Affirmation: I am doing my best in each moment.

6 of ENERGY

Freedom is more about letting go than having the option to hold on. Expansion alone does not make one free. Instead, true freedom comes from releasing what we think we need and the stories we create for ourselves.

Experience: Freedom

In our late teens and early twenties—when we start to live on our own, with some separation from parents and family—freedom is about getting to do what we want. By then, we have spent our life under the rules and watch of others, no doubt about it. *By God, I'm free at last*! is our mantra.

However, once we arrive at our thirties and forties, many find that they are not so free after all. We start to realize how attached we are to having our way. We need people to respect us; people to do as we say. I had a few clients in this age group tell me that if their mate didn't act as if they respected him or her, then he or she was done. Just like that. "I won't take their lack of respect." This isn't freedom. This is an attachment to expectations. When life doesn't go the way we want, how do we reconcile the gap between our expectations and reality?

Freedom is not being able to do what we want; freedom is being able to accept what is. The mature way to view freedom is *knowing* that freedom comes from accepting what is.

Many of us say, "I set my intentions. Now I demand the Universe give me what I want." Or, "See how free I am? I get to do whatever I want. And to hell with those who stand in my way."

I say, accept what comes. I am happy to go with the flow because giving up my opinions and what I perceive as my needs gives me a fuller feeling of receiving. When we release desires, anything we receive is satisfying and induces gratitude.

The difference is about the freedom to be, rather than the freedom to act however we want. The latter freedom is attachment to our egoistical needs. Freedom is like flying out of an open cage door and never looking back. Freedom is not needing to be right in discussions. Freedom is giving away things we might like because it makes someone else happy. "Here, take the thing I most treasure, I want you to have it."

Some people, even from an early age, can consider the needs of others. Those people sometimes need to learn to value their own needs. Others are allowed to be selfish or adapt to selfishness all on their own. It's a stage of life, and some of us never grow out of it.

How can we learn to live another way? It frequently takes a crisis of sorts. A time of pain and suffering during which we can clearly see our behaviors and the harm they cause ourselves and others.

We need to feel our own pain and the pain that arises in others. This is the great solvent that breaks up our attachments and the blindness they cause.

It's a perfect summer day. A light breeze and some shade keep it from becoming too hot.

Friends are preparing food, and there is an opportunity to go for a nice swim if you'd like. It's like your birthday. This is how freedom feels.

Let life come. It's not giving up our own opinions, but weighing life's offerings as greater. See freedom, not without externally imposed restraints, but without internally imposed restrictions. Enjoy the freedom of the day!

Significance: Jupiter in Leo, success, achievement, effort, persistence, impatience, fortune, competition, maturity, balance, awareness, gratitude, clear vision, delays, honesty

Lessons: The 6 of Energy is here to offer the rewards of success. But success needs to be earned through clear vision and honest effort. Living in true freedom will change how one views success. It becomes an inside job and not about any material success.

Practices: How do you see your own sense of freedom? In what ways do you restrict yourself? Explore the times when you felt truly free and without any needs.

Next Step: Allow the mind and body to live and enjoy life as it is.

Contemplate: Having an agenda about anything is not freedom.

Higher Octave: Free to be and do or not do.

Affirmation: I will stop holding myself back; I will be free and live feeling full.

7 of ENERGY

St. Francis of Assisi and Brother Leo share a story that touches all hearts. The stories themselves—the little flowers—were from Latin texts written about one hundred and fifty years after the death of St. Francis.

Experience: Overcoming Oneself

The joy we long for is not about being seen at the top of a mountain. True fulfillment is not about being recognized as the biggest or best. Letting go of the small self is not about having the most popular viewpoint. They're not about intentions or affirmations. They're not about what others think. They don't have an early bird special. They don't have four easy steps. They're not found by being on social media. They're not about rising above others.

Overcoming oneself comes from releasing all these ideas and embodying perfect joy.

There is a story that tells of Saint Francis of Assisi's perspective on perfect joy. It is over eight hundred years old and has been told many times in many ways. This version, quoted verbatim, is from a New Seed's 2006 translation by Robert Hopcke and Paul Schwartz.

How, on the road with Brother Leo, Saint Francis taught him concerning the things that make for perfect joy.

While making their way back home to Santa Maria degli Angeli from Perugia one winter, each of them suffering greatly from the extreme cold, Saint Francis called out to Brother Leo walking before him and said, "Brother Leo, even if the Friars Minor were to be known throughout the world as exemplars of holiness and wisdom, please understand—indeed, write it down in words—that such an accomplishment would not make for perfect joy."

Further along in their travels, Saint Francis called out to him a second time, saying, "Oh Brother Leo, even if the Friars Minor were to give sight to the blind, make the crooked straight, drive out demons, restore hearing to the deaf, make the lame to walk and the dumb to speak, indeed, even if they were able to raise the dead to life after four days—write it down in words—such accomplishments would not make for perfect joy."

Still further along the way, Saint Francis shouted out again, "Oh Brother Leo, if the Friars Minor knew all the languages of the world, were possessed of full knowledge of all things, and knew every last word of Scripture so as to prophesy and reveal, not just future things, but every secret in the conscience of every person on earth—write it down—even this would not make for perfect joy."

And again, as they continued, Saint Francis called out one more time, in a louder voice, "Oh Brother Leo, little lamb of God, even if the Friars Minor spoke the language of the angels and knew the courses of the stars in the heavens and the powers of every plant, if they were granted insight into every treasure of this world, and knew everything there was to know about every bird, fish, or animal, every stone, and every body of water upon the face of the earth, even then—write it down in words—all of this would not make for perfect joy."

A few steps further, Sanit Francis exclaimed, "Oh Brother Leo, even if the Friars Minor knew how to preach so powerfully as to convert every person on earth to a faith in Christ Jesus—write it down—it would not make for perfect Joy."

Hearing Saint Francis speak in this way for a good two miles, Brother Leo, with great admiration, finally asked him, "So holy Father, I beg you tell me then, on behalf of God, what *would* make for perfect joy?"

Saint Francis replied, "When we have arrived at Santa Maria degli Angeli, drenched in rain, frozen to the bone by the cold, covered in mud, dead with hunger, and when we knock on the door of the house and the doorman comes and asks us, 'Who is there?' and we say, 'We are two of your brothers,' and he answers us saying, 'You liars, you are nothing but a couple of cheating, thieving bandits going about the world stealing alms from the poor, get out of here,' closing the door in our face and sending us out into the wet snow to spend the night cold and hungry—when we then bear such insult, cruelty, and contemptuous treatment with patience, bearing the man no ill will nor saying a single word against him, thinking rather that it was God who led him to speak that way to us, oh Brother Leo—write it down in words—that would make for perfect joy.

"And if we were to knock yet one more time and he where to come to us, angry, swearing at us as if we were nothing but a pair of bothersome louts, driving us away by shouting, 'I told you to get out of here, you worthless thieves, go beg for your bread at the poorhouse. You aren't staying here or getting anything to eat out of us,' and we endure this mistreatment with patience, good cheer, and affection, oh Brother Leo—write it down in words—this makes for perfect joy.

"And if, overcome with hunger and cold, yet one more night we knock and ask for shelter, begging him for the love of God to open up and let us in, and yet a third time, furious, he says, 'I'll give these two obnoxious good-for-nothings what they deserve,' and comes after us with a big, knotted club, throwing us on the ground by our hoods and beating us on the ground in the snow with his club, all of which abuse we endure with patience and good cheer, thinking only of the sufferings of Christ and bearing our own suffering out of love for him , oh Brother Leo—write it down in words—this makes for perfect joy.

"But now, hear the conclusion, Brother Leo. Higher than all the graces and gifts granted by the Holy Spirit to Christ's beloved is the grace of self-mastery, willingly enduring pain, insult, contempt, and discomfort out of love for him. We cannot ourselves glory in any other gift from God, as the apostle said, 'What do you have that has not been given to you by God? And even given by God, why do you glory in it, as if it were your own doing?' But, if we endure the cross of our trials and afflictions willingly, in that we can glory, as the apostle has said, 'I will not glory but in the cross of our Lord Jesus Christ.'"

Praise be to Jesus Christ and to his poor servant Francis.

Amen.

Significance: Mars in Leo, courage, action, advancement, reevaluation, confrontation, challenges, anxiety, trust, forward moving, limitations, resistance, overcoming, progress

Lessons: The 7 of Energy is ready to make a stand on what is true. There will always be those trying to knock us off our spot, willing to create inner doubt. When we refuse to compromise on truth, we can stand firm even in a blizzard's wind.

Practices: What brings you perfect joy? What holds you back from living that truth? Share joy with others, without saying what your joy is.

Next Step: Be willing to be seen and not heard.

Contemplate: I can inspire others just as I have been inspired by others.

Higher Octave: I release others' opinions of me.

Affirmation: I will never give up.

8 of ENERGY

In India, while there is a great sense of gratitude among the people, there isn't an expectation to say thank you. It is assumed and expected that you would be there for a friend whenever they need you, so there is no need to be thanked. In fact, it would be offensive to say thank you to others, especially those closest to you.

Perhaps the tradition behind this comes from a famous and powerful mantra in the Upanishads:

matrudevo bhava, mitradevo bhava, pitrudevo bhava, putradevo bhava, acharyadevo bhava, atithidevo bhava

Translated literally, this mantra means, "Be one for whom the Mother is God, be one for whom the Friend is God, be one for whom the Father is God, be one for whom the Child is God, be one for whom the Teacher is God, and be one for whom the Guest is God."

"The Guest is God" is an attitude of respect and reverence for others that creates a solid foundation for living in gratitude.

Experience: Gratitude

I begin this theme on gratitude with feelings of thankfulness and appreciation. Gratitude is an excellent fine oil that can lubricate all our experiences and interactions to reduce friction among us and inside us. Gratitude is an inward feeling that *I have enough and am content*, even if only for a moment at a time.

I witnessed a memorable interchange between a teacher and a doubting student many years ago. "Well," the student said, "suppose I only had nine fingers. How could I feel gratitude?" The teacher responded, "I'd feel gratitude for the nine fingers,". The student continued. "But suppose I only had eight?" "Then I'd feel gratitude for the eight." "And five?" "Then I'd be happy for the five."

Gratitude, while we may go in and out of feeling it, doesn't have an on/off switch. We can't feel gratitude for some parts of our life and pissed about other parts. Well, I suppose we can, but I'm not sure that's real gratitude. There is a larger, more encompassing reality to gratitude.

Gratitude sees life's conditions from a step outside the day-to-day dramas. It takes a wide-angle view that is necessary for a healthy perspective. We can't have a sinking feeling while in gratitude. Gratitude is like taking a permanent vacation from our problems.

How do we embrace gratitude? Meditate on what we have—the things and experiences that others may not be so fortunate to have. Consider how far we have come in life. All challenges provided strength and experience. The unkind things we did are our friends too. They serve us, in the end, with teachings and guidance.

Feelings of gratitude may come and go until we solidify into a state of grace. When we're in grace, there's no reason to make any kind of story. Do we judge an apple in July because it is not ripe yet? Maybe some do, but I wouldn't. I feel happy in July that there are apples on the tree. Are there enough apples on the tree? Yes, there are, whatever *enough* means, because I feel gratitude.

Deep maturity is needed to feel gratitude on a heart-opening level. It isn't the kind of subject that a teacher would teach on the first day of school. We have to cozy up to it for the feelings to be real. Gratitude makes a great friend, because once we have it, we will always be thankful.

Significance: Mercury in Sagittarius, communication, resolution, removing obstacles, clarity, assurance, misunderstandings, jealousy, envy, holding back, authenticity, movement

Lessons: The 8 of Energy knows there are many challenging points along the path of life. Communicating with the world through finding our own authenticity can reduce any friction we meet. Then, opportunities abound in all directions.

Practices: Can you name a few things you're grateful for? Is there someone you admire because they have gratitude? Can you remember situations that seemed bad at first, but turned out good in the end? Use this lesson to bring gratitude to all situations in your life.

Next Step: Count your blessings.

Contemplate: Only I stop myself from taking action.

Higher Octave: I am always guided and protected.

Affirmation: I will break the bounds of whatever holds me.

9 of ENERGY

Living life as an offering is like offering flowers to someone—not anyone in particular—with long crazy arms and hands.

Experience: You're Easy to Love

We humans can be kind of inhumane to each other. We can be insensitive, show a lack of compassion, and be downright rude. Pets get better treatment than our neighbors. Many show more respect for their cars than their co-workers. It is possible to care more for our phone than for our relatives.

This inhumanity—often the result of ignorance and insecurity— feels painful on the receiving end. People will say things and act in ways that leave us feeling hurt and angry, even if we know better. We hold these pains for years and even decades—so long that we forget exactly who or what situation caused them. It's not unusual to be forty or older and still talk about pain from childhood. This is a common human story.

We can help each other with kind words and sensitivity. We can help ourselves by sharing heartfelt thoughts with others. Have we forgotten the effects of what we do and say on other people? Maybe we never knew. To share kindness shows strength and courage.

Years ago, I had a teacher say four words to me that wiped away years of pain. These words are still as supportive today as they were then. Those four words were, "You're easy to love."

In my own life, I held on to feeling different and misunderstood. I felt judged, even as I carried the capacity to judge others. I thought others were more spiritual and disregarded the power and loving feelings I possessed. Those four words wiped my doubts away. I've used these words on others over the years, and have told this story a few times. It seems like one of the best things we can do in life is to pass on support and love to others. It's wonderful to watch people grow and bloom.

When we get stuck in self-interest, we lose our ability to see and express the common good. We can't reach out beyond ourselves. That is what this theme is about. Let's work to find and use our voices to support and help others. It doesn't take much effort. Does it come from having a positive attitude? Yes, that helps. We need to avoid getting stuck in our own story and ways of thinking. When we live like that, our heads are buried in the sand.

"Do unto others as you would have them do unto you." This is from the Bible and is found in all religions in some form, but it isn't religious by nature. It became known as the Golden Rule. Another way to see it is, "Love your neighbor as yourself." Saying kind words and being sensitive to others is a sign of an open heart. It shows maturity; it radiates caring. The last step is to let others know what you see and how you feel, but not in a way that is intended to make them feel guilty or uncomfortable. We need to be sensitive to what others are feeling. Timing can be important.

"You look nice today," "I love your cooking," "It's nice to spend time with you," "I admire your abilities," "You touch my heart," "I love you." Want to change the world? Change yourself, reach out, and speak your heart. This will help us all feel that we are easy to love.

Significance: Sun in Sagittarius, wholeness, near completion, defending, unprepared, vulnerable, inner fears, self-knowledge, recuperating, latent power, strength, assurance

Lessons: The 9 of Energy has inner strength and ability gained through courage and learned through many challenges. There will be tests, so there is a natural inclination to be prepared. We can safely extend ourselves when we come from a place of balance and love.

Practices: What words and actions from others have held deep meaning or pain for you? Do you share your heart with others? How might your life change as you share your feelings?

Next Step: Learn to trust your inner guide.

Contemplate: I am always loved.

Higher Octave: Give to others what you wish to be given.

Affirmation: I am close to living my *truth*.

10 of ENERGY

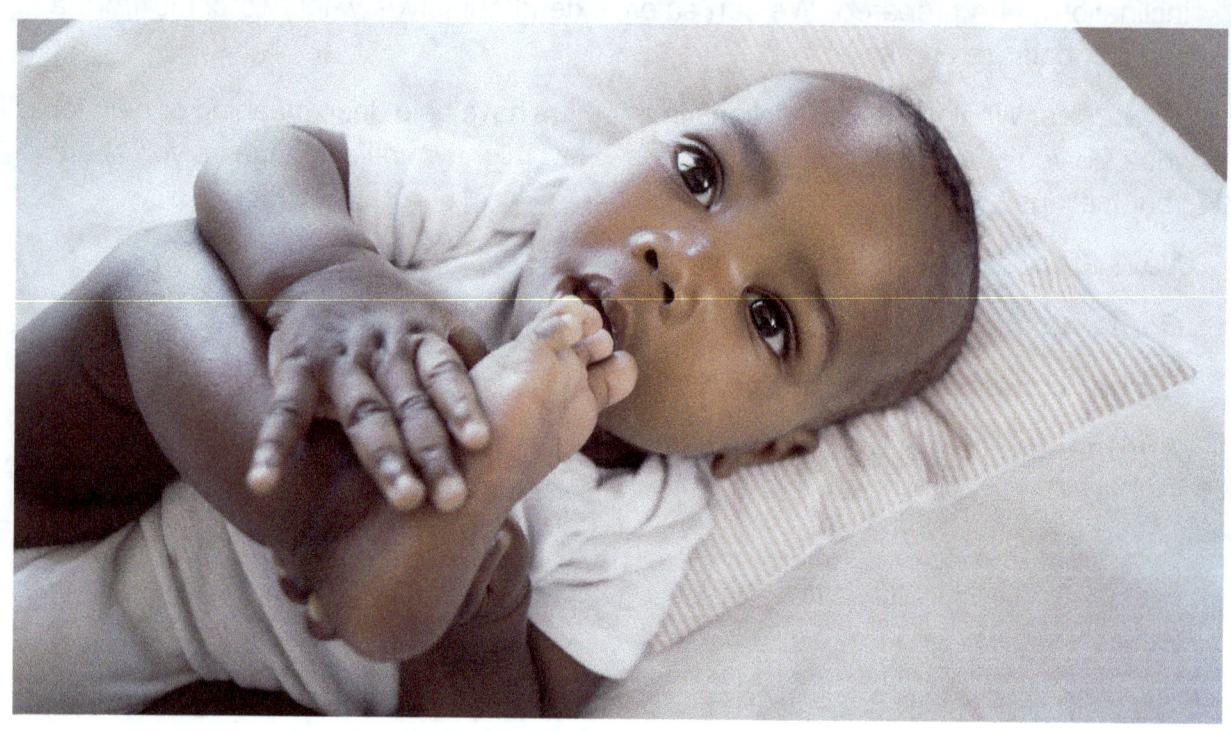

At three to six months old, the human baby grabs his or her foot. The baby doesn't know it's a foot or that it's theirs. While conditioning starts in the womb, at this age, humans are still pre-concepts.

Experience: 'I' ness

A year later, Mommy says, "Baby's blanket, baby's blanket." The plot thickens.

Six months later, the toddler says, "My blanket, my book, my mommy." Here in toddlerhood, we have assumed the mantle of 'I' ness. The misidentification has occurred. The misidentification is that we *think* we are an 'I' separate from others, but able to control the world. So, we spend the rest of our life learning that we are NOT the ego nor the mind.

'I' ness is a story. At first, it is fun, kind of like a favorite toy. It helps us to do stuff. It's entertaining, it's melodramatic, and it keeps us company. It gives us cycles and rhythm and makes meaning out of everything. The 'I' ness is kind of like a series of extreme Disney characters inside our head that bring aspects of our personality out to the world.

'I' ness is an identity formed of the body and self. It offers a kind of integration on the physical plane, but over time, it becomes inefficient. It gets in the way with its needs and desires. It doesn't offer real pleasures or happiness, only the kinds that don't last. It creates suffering through attachments, insecurities, and fears. When 'I' ness is in charge, it's a terrible way to live. It's like someone put a "maniac" at the helm.

In part 'I' ness originates from the use of "I" centered language that has been going on for thousands of years. It is possible to center language on objects (nouns) or actions (verbs), but the use of "I," "me," and "mine" (pronouns) means that we end up identifying with who we think we are rather than a deeper truth. This becomes the driving force.

Here is an example of how language can be altered to decentralize 'I' ness:

Pronoun: "I visit the tree," which is centered on the individual, not the tree.

Noun: "Tree," with no sense of 'I' ness attached.

Verb: "Treeing," which is being one with the tree.

It is apparent that we are separate from our mommy in that we have different bodies. She feeds us. She takes care of us. We experience her leaving us, though she does come back. These separate bodies give us the opportunity for individuality, which is a strong part of why we are here.

But, the reality is, we are all connected in mysterious ways. We can feel each other, we can know what others are thinking. We feel connection to others that goes beyond any rational understanding. Trees talk to each other through their roots. They can warn each other of dangers coming their way. We also have gifts like this.

We are neither our mind nor our body. It isn't *your* mind or *your* body. The mind and body just are, without ownership. It's not *my* peace, *my* joy, or *my* wisdom; it's about tapping into the highest Self, where *peace*, *joy*, and *wisdom* live, and accessing them there.

'I' ness fears dissolution through surrendering the illusion of a separate existence. It fears dissolving into nothing. But one's true reality is not a "who" (a pronoun again), but an Essence—a loving Allness—which is so much more comforting and fulfilling than the 'I' ness can ever be.

Who we are is Essence. It's the Knowing that, without bias or judgment, just seems to know the right answer to life's serious and mundane questions. If we all received proper education about who we really are and the true nature of life, we could all awaken to the nature of our own reality by eighteen years of age.

While the mind can be helpful for grocery lists and following directions, I haven't used it to make any decisions in my life for many years. I use *knowing* to figure out plans and directions. Even mundane decisions like where to eat out or what to eat at home can be made by the *knowing*, because in the *knowing* I never experience a "wrong" answer.

So, who are we? What is this 'I' ness? This is life's eternal question. Don't misidentify with being the thoughts or the ego, because that leads to suffering. Suffering arises when we are ruled by expectations and needs that lead us to live compulsively. Observe the 'I' ness, make friends with it, then let it go. When we live in each moment—not in the past or future—a natural peace engulfs us. When we feel connected to all, all questions disappear, including 'I' ness.

Significance: Saturn in Sagittarius, breakdown, breakthrough, too much responsibility, egotism, burdens, truth, attachments, expansion, new awareness, surrender, freedom

Lessons: There comes a time when truths need to be faced. The 10 of Energy wants us to make the highest decision at that time. *Knowing* who we really are, not who we think we are, is the way to proceed.

Practices: Can you imagine a peace so deep that wants and needs disappear? Do you experience feeling deeply connected to people around you? Attempt not to use the word "I" for a day or an hour. Or just notice when you use it.

Next Step: Observe the thoughts and behaviors.

Contemplate: I am happiest in simple pleasures.

Higher Octave: The freedom to let things be as they are.

Affirmation: One thing I have control over is the limitations I put on myself.

ACE of FLOW

The artist in the zone. Karen Carpenter had a rare ability to transition from the typical female range to a much lower, yet pure, register. Modern pitch monitoring software shows she hit the notes pitch-perfect, octave to octave. It was the quality of her voice that made her stsand out from the rest. Paul McCartney said, "She had the best female voice in the world; melodic, tuneful and distinctive." Elton John said, "She was one of the greatest voices in our lifetime."

Experience: The Artist

I don't listen to much music anymore. When I do, it's mostly old stuff that uplifts me and then, sometimes, songs on repeat. I've spent a whole year with a single album playing in the car or at home.

I've been listening and singing to Indian *bhajans*, or mantras, for most of my adult life. A mantra is a sacred sound or phrase believed to have spiritual power, mathematical structure, and deep meaning. They are repeated over and over, leading to a transcendental experience. They may contain our longing for the highest of human experiences—truth, love, and peace—or have a quality that evokes these sensations. That is probably why I listen continuously. It's not really a conscious act.

In India, I've been stuck on a Karen Carpenter song for two months and running. Right now, she is the inspiration.

Her voice merges with that mic and the oboe, making them one. I don't think she is singing the song her way. She is in "the zone"—another place where artists go when they are connected to a higher power, when the art is flowing through them instead of being of them. The arrangement is so meticulous; it flows completely naturally. The words disappear. I feel so complete with the three minutes and forty-six seconds that I don't hear it. But I feel it, and it becomes one with me. That is my experience.

Sometimes, on a creative level, we play the role of Karen. We are the artist expressing our flavor of energy. Sometimes we play the role of her brother, Richard, who does the arrangements, and plays the piano, yet also knows that his role includes getting out of the way.

Sometimes we are the audience, paying to see and appreciate. Participating in the energy in the hall or club is an important role. We have much to add. Sometimes we are the YouTube statistic, adding view counts that reward the artist. Each role is holy and needed. It's all art.

There is a motivation in life that is ultimately creative. By becoming the artist, the art, or the one experiencing the art, we are existing in a very special way. We are. We are expressing. We are alive.

At some point in our lives, we play all the roles in existence—art, artist, parent, child, or observer. Each is sacred when we see it that way. Any other attitude limits us and keeps us from appreciating the art of life.

Art speaks a wordless language. It nourishes our inner being. It gives us hope. It makes us smile and cry. It brings meaning where there may not have been any before. Life is not the same without it.

Enjoy the sunshine outside today. The Sun is dancing. The Moon loves to see our crooning and spooning. Amongst the winds, rivers, and birds, there is a lot of music. For me right now, Karen and I are one, over and over, speaking our special language of art and being the artist.

Significance: Creativity, emotional growth, freedom, open-hearted, selfish, self-focused, out of harmony, abundance, ambition, receptive, open channel, germinating seeds, nourishment

Lessons: The Ace of Flow says that every day is a new opportunity. We can show up our best by honoring the soulful expressions that flow through us. These expressions fill us and overflow to touch others.

Practices: How do you appreciate art in your life? How has art influenced you? What would your life be like without art?

Next Step: Recognize when you hold back your love and self-expression.

Contemplate: When you are afraid or doubting, give more.

Higher Octave: You can touch others more deeply with your way of being.

Affirmation: All doors and windows are open, as this is the time to be.

2 of FLOW

The path of the heart pulls me into it, like a spiral.
We go around and around but never come back to the same place.

Experience: The Path of the Heart

Recently, I was asked about my beliefs and teachings. Though I have teachers who teach Hinduism and Buddhism, I am not a Hindu or a Buddhist. Oh, I know some of the tenets—I quote them, teach them, and live them—but they are not me, or my way.

If I had to have a label, though I am not interested in being identified by any "ism," what fits the best is my own version of being on the path of the heart.

In my years of extensive travel, before smartphones and the internet were everywhere, I traveled with an iPod full of music. It contained mostly mantras or songs used for devotion. I even used my "regular" Western music as mantras.

I vividly remember listening to a few songs on repeat, staring out of windows while traveling across China, Mongolia, Eastern Europe, Peru, and all over Asia. Or walking and listening while my heart opened wide, crying my eyes out at the beauty of life contained in each tiny moment.

Can you live your life as if you are living in the tender moments we experience in our beloved movies? Take, for example, that scene with Tom Hanks and Meg Ryan when they finally get together at the end of *You've Got Mail.* There, in the park, meeting face-to-face, she says, "I wanted it to be you. I wanted it to be you so badly." Then they embrace, while "Somewhere over the Rainbow" plays in the background.

When we watch this scene, we are naturally in our hearts, not our heads. Can you live like "Somewhere Over the Rainbow" is playing in the background of your life? I have lived in this vulnerable loop for years. Seconds become minutes. Minutes become hours. Days become a lifetime. I was all alone but felt no separation from anyone or anything. I embraced my vulnerability to life, which is our reality, whether we choose it or not. I embraced authenticity. I developed courage. I was not interested or willing to live any other way. The Buddha said that once a person has heard of Enlightened Truth, they will never be satisfied with anything else.

Over that period, new perceptions overtook my old ones. I stopped seeing people and their problems. Instead, I saw beating hearts. I saw compulsions and compassions. I saw opportunity instead of challenge. People around me started seeing this in me, and naturally wanted to understand it. Even without their awareness, they started breaking down their own barriers upon seeing mine dismantled.

So how does one travel on this bus, dear friend? We find and live out of our heart. I practice presence. It never stops. It has developed beyond a practice into a lifestyle; a way to be, *the* way to be. I keep coming back to my feelings and my intuition. No judging, no right or wrong. I live in what is.

We need to develop the ability to see life through our hearts.

Be objective with yourself about how you live. Find your own song and put it on a loop. Be willing to be sentimental and even romantic. Admit what you can't admit. Open that internal closet and give it a good spring cleaning. Love what you can't love, then love it some more. Soon, others will see you differently. I'll meet you there, at the corner of vulnerability and open-heartedness.

Significance: Venus in Cancer, balance within, true friendship with self, equanimity, negative emotion, selfishness, unity, connection, communication, sympathy, self-love, perception

Lessons: We can't live our life looking for others to complete us and satisfy our needs. The 2 of Flow says open yourself fully and others will be open to you. This is how a true exchange becomes possible.

Practices: Do you admire people in your life who live from their heart? Study them, ask them how it is for them. What media or life experiences have touched your heart? Immerse in them for a whole weekend. Be honest with yourself about how your life is going. What would you like to change?

Next Step: Dare to be vulnerable.

Contemplate: I could live my whole life like this.

Higher Octave: In each moment, surrender to what is.

Affirmation: I am ready for joy and fulfillment.

3 of FLOW

The breakup. At first, we are heartbroken.
Later, we rediscover ourselves. We experience simple pleasures again, maybe for the first time in a long time.
We learn not to fear change. The simpler the life, the better.
Then we meet the real one, and we realize how much we gained through the process.

Experience: Addition by Subtraction

Addition by subtraction is a phrase popularized in the sporting world as a way to explain the phenomenon when quality players get injured, yet the team starts playing better overall. We also see this happen when certain practice exercises are cut from a team's routine, or even when a coach is fired.

Addition by subtraction is when we lose or give up things we thought were essential, only to experience improvements even with those subtractions.

A breakup of a relationship, as mentioned above, is another example. First, we feel the subtractions in the breakup. This might include the loss of a friend and lover, the loss of companionship, the loss of joy and the pain of having been hurt by someone we loved, and the loss of confidence. Finally, after embracing the pain, we get to a point of healing in which we learn to love ourselves. We acknowledge that we do have value and self-worth. We can love others again, this time appreciating the experience of love and ourselves even more. In the end, we have gained more than we lost.

We can also find addition by subtraction in our business environments. In corporate takeovers, the incoming organization is betting on addition by subtraction when it lets go of 10 percent or 20 percent of the workforce. How about remote working—bosses lose control and workers leave the office and work from home, enhancing productivity and improving morale. Some employees end up working more than before.

More doesn't always mean better.

Addition by subtraction isn't a new idea in the spiritual world. Let's go back 2,500 years to Lao Tzu, the great Chinese philosopher, when he wrote this verse:

Thirty spokes share the wheel's hub,
It is the center hole that makes it useful.
Shape clay into a vessel,
It is the space within that makes it useful.
Cut the doors and windows for the room,
It is the holes which make it useful.
Therefore, profit comes from what is there,
Usefulness from what is not there.

In essence, he said:
To attain knowledge, add things every day.
To attain wisdom, subtract things every day.

Profit comes from what is there, and
Usefulness comes from what is not there.

Spiritually, we all love to go for the gold—the highest vibration. We get our intentions all juiced up. But they, gold and intentions, don't make us happy; we make us happy. There is always something more to find. When we subtract what does not serve us, we quicken our path because what is left is perfect.

Don't be small-minded; be larger-minded. The Bible tells us the meek shall inherit the earth. Spiritually, we can view addition as having an egotistical component. Subtraction, on the other hand, contains humility and surrender.

This is the 80/20 rule in action, the universal truth about the imbalances of inputs and outputs. When we remove the things we don't want from life—which is the 20 percent (such as anger or fear) —we make room for the things in life that we do want—the 80 percent (love and peace). Spiritually, when we release what we believe but isn't true, this will lead to the most direct way to reach a higher state, through the practice of addition by subtraction.

Significance: Mercury in Cancer, growth, happiness, communication, freedom, pettiness, overindulgence, uncentered, emotional, sharing, perfection, substance, full expression

Lessons: We view most of life's experiences through a lens of success or failure. The 3 of Flow says that those words have little meaning. In each moment, we experience exactly what we are supposed to experience.

Practices: Have you had an experience of addition by subtraction? Did things go as you expected? Experiment with releasing someone or something from your life, and experience if you feel addition and/or subtraction.

Next Step: Appreciate what we have in each moment.

Contemplate: The honeymoon stage is living in happiness and unhappiness.

Higher Octave: I am free to add or subtract.

Affirmation: I am available for whatever life gives me.

4 of FLOW

Experience is a great teacher.
Sometimes, instead of locking the fox out of the henhouse,
we lock it in. The fox is our avoidance, thoughts,
and attitudes that cover up real feelings (the chickens).
We close ourselves off to soft, vulnerable feelings because
we fear being overwhelmed by them. Then we engage in
unnecessary drama to create proof of the world's dangers
from which we require self-protection.

Experience: Everything We Tell Ourselves is from the Mind

When we tell our stories, we are protecting the fox, not the chickens.
When we defend anything, we are holding a position.
When we hold a position, we are coming from ego.
Coming from ego is suffering.
Ego must be held to exist.
Ego and awareness cannot co-exist.
Bring awareness to what is happening now.
See what ego is there.

The Truth we feel inside us and around us—what we *know* without trying to know—cannot be experienced in the mind.

In fact, the mind keeps Truth away.

It can take ten to twenty years from the first pre-awakening experiences to get to awakening.

The level of meticulousness necessary to get to *truth* is extreme.

How does the mind comprehend this?

It doesn't. That's why we spend day after day being humbled by life.

Bring awareness to what is happening now. See what ego is there. Bringing awareness to the stories we tell ourselves will dissolve them. Then we become unstuck from everything.

Significance: Moon in Cancer, lack of stability, holding back, reflection, disgust, joy, creativity, discontent, emotions, peace, assurance, content, knowing, freedom

Lessons: The ups and downs of life can wear us down. The 4 of Flow holds the power to reverse lifelong patterns of behavior. In recognizing how we cause ourselves pain, we find solutions.

Practices: Are the stories you tell yourself true? Can you trace the origin of these stories? Allow yourself freedom from these stories, if only for a minute.

Next Step: Find your own *truth* and hold on to it. Write it down and make it special.

Contemplate: When I stop listening to the mind, I feel happier.

Higher Octave: I am not the stories I tell myself.

Affirmation: I have the power to believe and disbelieve anything.

5 of FLOW

A key to loving yourself is to open your heart.
What is it like to have the heart open?
Until it is experienced, one can't really know.

Experience: I Trusted Once, and I Got Hurt

"I trusted once, and I got hurt." I heard these words from a beautiful, innocent young woman. It became kind of a theme for a season in India as people explored their hearts being closed.

I've come to think that, for many of us, there is a moment between ages two and nine —or perhaps a series of moments—when our innocence is shattered by experiences that we interpret as ultimate pain. Thus, we feel we need to close our hearts to protect ourselves. We become frozen in a moment in time. Frozen by a concept, that was true then, but is not always true.

What we don't realize is that the pain of a closed heart is much greater than the pain of hurt feelings. When we live with a closed heart, we get into bad relationships, fighting, disagreements, and isolation. We don't trust nature. What a cosmic joke. We don't trust the life that exists before and after our being here.

Sperm and ovum meet, and a baby is created. We forget to think about what a miracle that is. Trust is an important skill to develop in our life. To trust that we are supported and that the right events happen takes dedication and time spent working on ourselves.

Every day is a new beginning all over the world. Learn to turn the page to a higher presence and joy in your life by living with an open, available heart. Trust again, even if you get hurt.

Significance: Mars in Scorpio, disappointment, challenges, disruption, emotion, despair, sacrifice, new confidence, appreciation, refocus, take action, sober, eye to eye, transformation

Lessons: Life does not always go as we plan or hope, but each experience is an opportunity to learn and grow. The 5 of Flow encourages us to explore our feelings of disappointment. What we find there can change our life for the better.

Practices: What is love? What do we learn from our feelings of disappointment? When love is present, do you feel isolated?

Next Step: Be honest with yourself.

Contemplate: Appreciate what we have, even when times are tough.

Higher Octave: Expectations lead to disappointments.

Affirmation: I am guided and protected in each moment.

6 of FLOW

Rishikesh, a city in Northern India, sits beautifully in the Himalayan foothills, beside the Ganga River. Temples and ashrams line the banks, and the area is renowned as a center of meditation and the yoga capital of the world. The Rishikesh walking bridges, which cross over the Ganga, are at the heart of the Rishikesh experience. In crossing the bridges, one experiences instant anxiety in a way I've never seen anywhere else. There is so much going on, we are in this experience together, it seems your whole life is passing in front of your eyes. Regular rules don't seem to apply there. Being in Rishikesh feels like your parents are away for the weekend all the time!

Experience: The Random Walk

Life in India can be challenging, but in very different ways than we experience in the West. And when you are in India, the West doesn't make much sense. India is a very different kind of place.

In all of India, there is noise, dirt, crowds, and traffic. To visitors, it appears to be chaos. There are motorbikes everywhere, cows in the streets, and the sounds of barking dogs and loud wedding music late into the night. Indians would not tell other Indians to tone it down.

In Rishikesh, all the traffic noise and chaos of the streets become greatly compressed onto Lakshman Jhula[1], a six-foot- wide, four- hundred- and- fifty-foot- long iron suspension bridge that hangs fifty feet above the holy river Ganga. Though there is two-way traffic, it' is not clear which side is which.

On the bridge, there are all sorts of users: cows, donkeys, monkeys, locals, tourists, and motorbikes. During the bridge crossing, you can find cows standing or resting on the bridge with no regard for lanes or blockage, cow dung, Indian tourists taking scenic selfies, professional photographers posing walkers across both sides of the bridge, monkey hanging on suspension wires looking for food to steal, large carts full of goods, and all the continually honking motorbikes. In this chaos, there are also beggars sitting to the side, silently holding cups for rupees.

When crossing, you learn to move quickly when there is open space, and you do not come out the same person as you started. It is a deeply affecting experience—one that is fun and exhilarating, and seems to last a lifetime.

One day, while crossing the very crowded bridge, I realized that Indians walk with complete unpredictability like molecules. You never know how they will move in crowds, making the crowds hard to navigate. In the utter chaos of the bridge, one calls out for some sense of order. This is why the India experience changes us on such a deep level.

This unpredictability reminds me of a scientific process called random walk, which consists of a sequence of discrete steps of fixed length, where the direction of each step is random and does not depend on the previous steps. This is the way molecules move.

By the same randomness, Indians refuse to move in predictable ways. What happens next doesn't necessarily have to do with what happened before. Random is important in this context because it teaches us to be in the present moment and to appreciate what we have. These are the lessons we learn every time we cross the bridge.

---

1   At the time of the writing of this theme, the Lakshman Jhula was still in operation, However, it was closed in 2019 due to safety concerns. They are now building a new, wider bridge next to it.

In chaotic environments like this, worldly concerns disappear. They seem small compared to what the Universe provides us each moment. There is time to explore the inner world and big questions like, *Who am I*? I spend months in India digging deep and then deeper. I ponder questions such as: What do I want to say? How can I help others? Am I fulfilled and complete as I am?

How do we live more deeply wherever we are, even if we're not gifted the opportunity to travel to places like India? These are the questions we may want to explore:

Can we disbelieve some of our own thinking?
Can we stop our own topsoil—our *truth*—from eroding?
Can we stop the neurological cascades in our minds?
Can we create new neural pathways,; new ways of acting and being?
Can we be like primitive molecules and bring a sense of randomness into our nature and movements, getting out of our conditioned thinking and behaviors, and becoming freer in action and thought?
Can we live free as a song, singing forever?

To live this way:

We need to spend time alone.
We need to spend time alone in nature.
We need to learn to be direct and honest in our communication.
We need to tune into our intuition for healing energies, and to receive information and guidance.
We need to know that it is not *our* vibration, it is just vibration, just like it is not *our* energy or *our* power.
We need to understand that we control nothing.
We need to feel the web of life that connects everything.
We need to allow ourselves to take the random walk.

Significance: Sun in Scorpio, innocence, harmony, rigidity, freedom, spontaneity, sensitivity, sitting in the past, sharing, homeland, maturity, transformation, rebirth, the eagle's eye

Lessons: Past events can fill us with joyous memories, like the feeling of returning home after being away for a long time. The 6 of Flow reminds us to live like this whenever we want to, wherever we are. In the present moment, by subtracting extra, we are left with what we were always looking for.

Practices: In what ways do you hold ideas that are not ultimately beneficial? How can a lowly molecule teach us humans anything? Do you recall times you got stuck in your head trying to understand something that was not understandable?

Next Step: Incorporate more randomness into your daily life.

Contemplate: If I hold myself rigid, I won't have the ability to flow.

Higher Octave: Give yourself up to satisfying energies around you.

Affirmation: I flow more freely the freer I am.

7 of FLOW

Fear of failure can paralyze us when we believe things that may not be true. If we can come to a place of center, we can see that fear is worse than failure. Then we are well on the way to healing.

Experience: Fear of Failure

Hosting a fear of failure is like having a ton of bricks dropped on you. It's like putting your finger in an electrical outlet and having a bucket of water thrown at you. But we do this to ourselves. Okay, our parents may imprint us with a failure button, but it's our choice to keep pressing it. Fear of failure can also be a self-fulfilling prophecy (5 of Energy). The more we fear, the more likely we are to fail. There are two aspects at work here: fear and failure. Let's examine them individually.

Fear, on the deepest level, develops to protect the body for primal security. It has great value on this primal level for a primal lifestyle. But we don't live on that level now, and our modern fears are generated from conditioned ideas that our minds generate in error. Things like being stuck in traffic or failing to finish a work project on time can feel threatening to our primal security. However, these experiences merely harm our expectations, not our physical body.

Fear is natural. But, as we grow, things or actions that were fearful become ordinary and mundane. Once we learn to swim, the swimming pool is not scary. We don't like to be alone driving in the car. Later, we wish we could be alone on all our outings. I hope that you learn to see fear as your friend. Fear is an indication of the truth you feel and areas of challenge. Fear is trying to teach us something.

Failure, on the other hand, is not actually possible. Failure is just a mental concept. What we call failure is just a stage on the continuum of living a life from birth to death. Even if we experience a failure, it is not a permanent state or anything to be ashamed of. Far from it. Failure builds character, encouraging us to be vulnerable and humble. And what joy it brings when turned to success! Think of failure as "not yet" rather than "never". Bring more determination to any situation. Know that you are still love and lovable, regardless of failure or success.

Fear of failure is natural. But what we do with that fear is our choice. The more we fear failure, the more likely we are to fail. Start seeing failure for what it is: a first step in success. Then we can let go of our fear of failure.

Significance: Venus in Scorpio, indecision, faults, unsure, indulging, escapism, new goals and ventures, follow through, taking action, roller coaster, perception, self-acceptance, reality

Lessons: We can only succeed in our goals when we believe in our abilities. The 7 of Flow is here to guide us when we bottom out. As we recognize what hinders us, we gain power over the shadows.

Practices: How do you act or think when you are afraid of failing? Think back to a time you were afraid. How did it work out in the end? *Knowing* that you don't know is true wisdom.

Next Step: Stop judging yourself by not listening to the mind.

Contemplate: In any situation, I can learn and grow and do the best that I can at that time.

Higher Octave: All situations are neutral.

Affirmation: I believe in my ability to overcome and be successful.

8 of FLOW

In his book, Walden, Henry David Thoreau wrote,
"I went to the woods because I wished to live deliberately, to front only
the essential facts of life, and see if I could not learn what it had to
teach, and not, when I came to die, discover that I had not lived.
I wanted to live deep and suck all the marrow of life."

Experience: Needs and Desires

Much of our life is centered around satisfying our needs and desires. This is an endless, cyclical game because needs create more needs, and desires, even when satisfied, appear again over time.

There are basic needs. A life in a body requires food, water, shelter, and finances. However, the wise one looks at how needs feed desires and desires feed needs. When we are stuck in limited thinking, we don't know that we can do things differently.

There is an old Indian teaching story that I've heard told a few different ways. The message is the same in all versions.

There was a simple monk who was sitting under a tree with his few worldly possessions, when a villager passed by and commented on the visible hole in the monk's outfit. The monk said, "Mice have eaten my loincloth." The villager said, "You need a cat to protect you. I'll get you one, and everything will be okay."

The villager gave him a cat. Weeks later, the monk was sitting under another tree and another villager passed by him. The villager said, "If you had a cow, you wouldn't need to beg for food— you'd have milk for you and the cat. I have an extra cow that I would be happy to give you." The monk thanked him for his offer. Subsequently, the simple monk acquired land to feed the cow, and a wife and children to help work the land. Before he knew it, the monk was caught in a storm of needs and desires. Eventually, he returned to his monastery to acquire his simple, unburdened life again.

Attachments to needs and desires hinder us. Simple preferences are not sticky and do not create the physical tensions that attachments create. It takes wisdom and insight to see through our predicaments. It is not easy to unravel the "why" of what we want. Furthermore, the moods we develop when we don't get our way cloud our thinking and feelings.

Needs and desires slip away when we live consciously. There may be things we would like, but we develop boundaries on what we are willing to give up for them. Then, we see desires as separating us from our *self*. We live a life of contentment and are less susceptible to being swayed out of our grounded positions for something that we know is not ultimately satisfying. When we live this way, we live from flow instead of needs and desires.

Significance: Saturn in Pisces, disenchantment, emotional disappointment, stagnation, change, freedom, new pursuits, fulfillment, growth, quest, higher calling, focus, discipline

Lessons: Too much unconscious living will eventually lead to dissatisfaction. The 8

of Flow offers clarity. With clarity comes resolution. Old behaviors disappear as we focus and set conscious limits.

Practices: Is what you think you need and desire really what you are seeking? Can you think of examples in your life when needs and desires created a feeling of being off center? What would happen if you were content with what you have right now?

Next Step: Living honestly and in integrity with our highest Self.

Contemplate: What brings real inner happiness?

Higher Octave: Live without expectations, grateful for what is and what you have now.

Affirmation: To live happily, be happy with simple.

9 of FLOW

L. Frank Baum, the author of The Wizard of Oz was a talented writer and actor who had a colorful career in newspapers, magazines, and on the stage. He was a man of deep convictions—truly ahead of his time—and his books contained his strong political and religious viewpoints. Modern writers suggest that the main characters' experiences in Oz are symbolic of the soul's journey toward Enlightenment by following the Yellow Brick Road (which can be interpreted as the Golden Path, the soul's journey toward Enlightenment). Baum himself said, "It was pure inspiration. It came to me right out of the blue. I think that sometimes the Great Author had a message to get across and He was to use the instrument at hand."

Experience: There's No Place Like Home

The 1939 adaptation of the first Oz book became a landmark 20th Century Studio's film. In the film, Dorothy, a young girl from Kansas, and her house are magically taken by a tornado to the Land of Oz, where the house lands right on top of the Wicked Witch of the East, killing her. The witches' ruby slippers appear on Dorothy's feet through the efforts of Glinda, the Good Witch of the North, who tells Dorothy not to take the ruby slippers off, as they are very powerful. Dorothy spends the rest of the movie having great adventures and trying to figure out a way to get back home, all while protecting the shoes.

After Dorothy accidentally kills the Wicked Witch of the West, who was fully committed to reclaiming her sister's ruby slippers, the movie draws to its conclusion with this dialogue:

Dorothy: Oh, will you help me? Can you help me?

Glinda: You don't need to be helped any longer. You always had the power to go back to Kansas.

Dorothy: I have?

Scarecrow: Then why didn't you tell her before?

Glinda: She wouldn't have believed me. She had to learn it for herself.

Scarecrow: What have you learned, Dorothy?

Dorothy: Well, I...I think that it, that it wasn't enough just to want to see Uncle Henry and Auntie Em...and that's it. If I ever go looking for my heart's desire again, I won't look any further than my own backyard. Because if it isn't there, I never really lost it to begin with! Is that right?

Glinda: That's all it is.

Scarecrow: But that's so easy! I should've thought of it for you.

Tin Man: I should have felt it in my heart.

Glinda: No, she had to find it out for herself. Now those magic slippers will take you home in two seconds!

Dorothy: Oh! Toto, too?

Glinda: Toto, too.

Dorothy: Now?

Glinda: Whenever you wish.

...

Glinda: Then close your eyes and tap your heels together three times. And think to yourself, "There's no place like home."

We always have what we need. And when we look outside ourselves for it, we will ultimately find that it was inside us all along. We have a brain, we have a heart, and we have bravery.

203

We can go home at any time.

This is a powerful metaphor for our own life. The question to ask isn't, *How can I meet a Good Witch who will give me magic shoes*? A better question to consider is, *How can I find these truths for myself*? Just remember to close your eyes and tap your heels together three times. And think to yourself, *There's no place like home.*

Significance: Jupiter in Pisces, attainment, satisfaction, accomplishment, patience, adventure, arrival, mistakes, imperfections, truth, loyalty, liberty, overindulgence, gluttony

Lessons: Situations of life are put in front of us for our own growth. The 9 of Flow reminds us to appreciate what we have and to recognize our own gifts. All is harmony and balance when we live in peace.

Practices: Go with the Flow. Let things be as they are. How do you react when things don't go the way you want them to? Do you live part of your life somewhere over the rainbow?

Next Step: Follow the yellow brick road.

Contemplate: Each moment is filled with harmony and joy.

Higher Octave: Everything we need is provided.

Affirmation: I am content, and fortune surrounds me.

10 of FLOW

*Color brings so much to our life in such a simple way.
Humble by nature, color expresses its truth and its vibration for all to
see. In a flower, in a special dress, or splashed about in nature,
color quietly makes us feel.*

Experience: Color

I read an interesting fact in *A Brief History of Time* by Stephen Hawking, and it just won't leave me alone. [1]

"The frequency (or number of waves per second) of light is extremely high, ranging from four to seven hundred million million waves per second. The different frequencies of light are what the human eye sees as different colors, with the lowest frequencies appearing at the red end of the spectrum and the highest frequencies at the blue end."

A hundred million million per second. Let's appreciate those colors! Compare that to what we get done in a day, let alone a second.

A mystical teacher (1 Magician) taught me that our personalities also have frequency and vibration. Each personality point has its own flavor, or color. We radiate our story. I read recently that if we knew how to read faces, we could see everyone's character and fate because it is contained there.

The realms of possibilities in the physical world are totally mind blowing when we think about it. When we add in other planes of existence, we start to comprehend just how small we are.

Humans are kind of in the middle of tiny and huge. Middle kids can feel kind of lost. But I'm of the mind that this is a place of sacred honor for humans. When we can use our minds for their highest purpose, we feel magically connected to all of existence. All musicians use the same eight notes on the musical scale, but just a few make music that is listened to for centuries. All artists use brushes and colors. But relatively few paintings hang in famous museums. What do you think is the difference?

The fact above about color is probably high school level science. But it touched me because I saw it in my heart, not in my head. Every book and article contain opportunity for creative expression. Every tree and flower can be immortalized by a lyric or oil painting. Every moment is ripe to be expressed. A simple spark of creativity is all that is needed to create. We don't need to vibrate billions of times a second to add color to our lives. The cosmic intelligence gives us light to take care of that. Color is already there.

---

1   Hawking, Stephen. *A Brief History of Time. Bantam Dell Publishing Group*, 1988. p. 38.

Significance: Mars in Pisces, abundance, protection, satisfaction, discontentment, anxiety, belonging, rainbows, freedom, radiating, secrets, completion, family, wholeness, doubts, joy

Lessons: We can look outside us to bring us to happiness. The 10 of Flow says to open our eyes to all, right here and now. Then, from our sensitive actions in the moment, joy will exist.

Practices: Think about times you have been creative. How did it feel? Do you have methods of limiting the colors in your life? Love what you do and who you are.

Next Step: Release the concept of next step.

Contemplate: The colors make the rainbow.

Higher Octave: Live like nothing is extra.

Affirmation: I come in colors everywhere; I'm like a rainbow.

ACE of INTELLIGENCE

A tortoise beats a hare in a race—an old Aesop fable.
The hare was overconfident and gave little to no effort, while the tortoise remained persistent and gave all his effort toward the goal. The same is true on a spiritual journey. Effort can take you far.

Experience: Spiritual Effort Needed

All spiritual seekers have moments of doubt on their journey. It is unclear exactly how one should attain spiritual goals because the goals and methods differ for everyone and can change as one progresses. This lack of clarity can be unsettling at times.

What are examples of spiritual goals? For some, practicing yoga consistently once a week is enough. Others pursue daily spiritual study and meditation to achieve a needed uplift. Some people are active in spiritual groups, focusing on service and a social element. Some dedicate their life to a guru. Others dedicate themselves to attaining Enlightenment or Awakening.

Wherever you fall on this spectrum, effort is required to *realize* goals on the spiritual path. Realize can mean to achieve them or to live them on deeper levels. The renowned Indian master Paramahansa Yogananda said, "The effort needed is 50% God's grace, 25% Guru's blessing (guidance and taking up of karma), and 25% disciple's part. But 100% effort is needed on the disciple's 25%."

Our 100% needs to be a full effort—complete, unwavering, conscious—to the best of our ability at any time. If we don't have a guru, life will act as one until we can access our inner guru.

The idea of "grace" has many meanings. In this context, it is a sensibility outside our normal being, enhancing our lived experiences. It's *knowing* we are always doing our best, even when that best doesn't feel great. We could think of grace as greater than ourselves, but grace *is* ourselves when we expand to meet it. Sometimes we see grace in the rear-view mirror, revealing itself after an experience has unfolded—for example, something done for us unexpectedly to alleviate a situation we worried would worsen. After some practice, we can understand it in real time that we are protected. On our journey, it's important to have this understanding. There will be setbacks, moments of hesitation, and perceived failure when we forget what we *know*. When these moments come up, grace is the answer.

Still, we need to do our best when working towards our spiritual goals. Some feel we need to live like the Olympic figure skater, dedicating ten to twenty years of life for only a few moments of performance under the lights. The prescribed diets, merciless schedules, and hours of precision practice are all necessary elements in this single-pointed focus.

I am not like the dedicated Olympian, certainly not with that kind of austere discipline. But I live with a sincere focus on higher principles of life. I have never lost sight of an unknown goal that eventually became to live righteously. Over time, I have doubted teachers and paths, but I've never lost the determination to go full throttle for what I was driven to do and then be. I listened and observed. I had a kind of arrogance to do it my way, not because my way was better, but because something in me fueled my determination to keep digging inside for my polished diamond. I never knew or cared what that diamond was, and I always trusted that it would be revealed when I could see it.

One of the beauties of life is that we are all different. Each one of us must find our core strengths and weaknesses. What do we have to give? What elements are missing? This is what we do. We must figure it out for ourselves, separate from (but supported by) the guru's insight and wisdom.

There is no single right answer for all! Maybe this path of inquiry *is* the spiritual journey. I reached a goal I didn't know I had. I believe not having the goal helped me to attain it because the goal was beyond my prior capacity to conceive it. Thus, my expectations couldn't limit or confuse me. The experience may or may not be the same for you.

No matter how your spiritual path is oriented, the effort needed is complete. The tortoise in the story teaches us that consistency and persistence win the race.

Significance: Initial thrust, enthusiasm, balance, caution, power, overcoming, determination, insurmountable problems, willpower, strength, courage, motivation, divine inspiration

Lessons: It's natural to be optimistic and assured at the beginning of any venture. The Ace of Intelligence reminds us that tests strengthen us; they do not shame us for insufficiencies. Strength comes from our dedication to sustain our path.

Practices: Can you see your spiritual goals? How have they changed over the years? Take one insight from this theme and work on it every day for a week.

Next Step: Realistically and honestly assess your effort in life.

Contemplate: All of life supports my efforts.

Higher Octave: I trust my perceptions.

Affirmation: Where there is a will, there's a way.

2 of INTELLIGENCE

The aerial roots of the amazing banyan tree grow downward from the main stem and branches. These roots are known as prop roots. They serve as pillars, supporting the massive horizontal branches of tree. In the same way, the inner guru helps support us through our expansive spiritual growth.

Experience: The Inner Guru

When we lead an aware life, mentors and teachers are everywhere. Books, articles, podcasts, and YouTube videos are among our most important possessions and guides. Perhaps we have the blessing of a guru, or a guru-like relationship in which we literally or figuratively sit at someone's feet in awe.

Whether you have a guru or not, we all need to recognize and learn to work with another important teacher.

That special teacher—the one all teachers should ultimately send us to—is the inner guru. Outer teachers and experiences can only take us so far. The wise teacher will encourage us to find and use our own intuition and wisdom. We all have these innate abilities, but for many, they need to be developed and explored.

The inner guru is a sense of *knowing* that exists inside us. We find it in stillness. It is not experienced as an achievement; it is not an accomplishment that the ego attains. It appears in the surrender of our being a person. What we *are* becomes clear. In that clarity, we can hear the Universe talking to us. The Universe is always talking to us, but until we learn how to *hear* it, we cannot experience it.

We must get quiet to access the inner guru. Quiet means being silent, and still in body and mind. The quiet inside will yield a remembrance—a connection to something bigger inside us. We touch the Essence of what we are. I feel this in an area near my stomach.. After working with the inner guru for a while, we will learn to see that Essence is not "ours." We do not possess it; it simply exists.

The process of developing our connection to the inner guru goes something like this. At first, we work hard to get quiet enough to experience the inner guru, even if just for a moment at a time. These rare moments will come as we open our hearts and stop listening to our minds. Then, we learn to put together the moment-to-moment experiences of true intuition and surrender. It becomes easier to access this place; less effort is required to achieve this state over time. Then the seesaw tips, and we live more in the inner *knowing* than we do in the "normal" life of chatter and mental impulses. Finally, the *knowing* becomes our new normal, and the mind chatter, doubting, and anxiety become rare and immediately recognizable.

We access the inner guru through an ability to live in contemplation. In learning to focus, moment-to-moment, we live without anything disturbing our spiritual path. We live like life is the giant trunk of a banyan tree, and we are one of the individual roots. The truth is, despite having a sense of being separate, we are part of the whole, and our roots buried in the ground, nurture the tree. The connection we experience with the whole of the tree is the inner guru.

Significance: Moon in Libra, emotional balance, inner peace, sensitive, justice, cooperation, partnership, stubborn, passivity, concentration, focus, freedom, inspiration, fullness

Lessons: Doubts and emotions block intuition and lead to passivity. The 2 of Intelligence says there is an inner peace that reveals all. With each step, we become closer to hearing the call of the Divine.

Practices: Have you experienced the *knowing* from inner wisdom? How do you bring stillness into your life? Imagine that you and the people around you are connected, like all the parts of one big banyan tree.

Next Step: Explore the feelings of calm and clarity.

Contemplate: I am the inner guru.

Higher Octave: I find the balance between intuition and emotions.

Affirmation: I am stable in the winds of life.

3 of INTELLIGENCE

Life is not as simple or dualistic as good and bad. Everything changes and produces consequences. When my kids were young, I was asked if my children were planned. My answer was, "Yes, they were planned, but not by us." I feel the same way about the rest of life. There is a plan, but I have no idea what it is.

Experience: Climate Change

The consequences of the last one hundred years of fourfold world population growth due to the rapidly increased production and technological advances are staggering.

On the one hand, we have experienced many wonderful benefits. We travel freely and explore the wonders of the Earth, have incredible tools for communication, and maintain scientific knowledge that helps us live longer. We live with greater ease, eat our favorite foods all year round, and have access to immediate satisfaction of our needs and wants. Distance and time have much less effect on us than they did a hundred years ago.

Conversely, changing weather, warming seas, polluted air and water, poisons in our food, and epidemics in health and drug use are powerful forces in our lives and the lives of our children. They are issues we will need to deal with for the rest of this twenty-first century, along with other worldwide catastrophes that likely lie ahead.

So, what is a conscious person to do about these realities in the physical plane world? I wonder this myself. We can't take the difficulties personally. We can't say it is only about us. We also can't ignore our responsibilities. We must learn to see life in bigger, less dense ways. Is it possible that this is the point of what we are experiencing?

Ken Wilber suggests that:

"It's not that harming the biosphere will eventually catch up with us and hurt us from the outside. It's that the biosphere is literally internal to us, is a part of our very being, our compound individually—harming the biosphere is internal suicide, not just some sort of external problem."[1]

The only "religion" that is truly free of dogma is nature. There is nothing in our life like the natural world. Go outside and worship. Worship the interconnectedness at the core of life. Worship the beautiful flowers and trees that grace this planet. Honor that we are here together. Honor that we are made from the same base ingredients. Honor that we feed each other. Honor the powerful, awe-inspiring symbiosis that is Earth.

We live in a world with a changing climate. The politics and greed surrounding these issues create an escalation of worldwide tensions that, in turn, lead to tensions inside us. This is what we must deal with. Will governments get it together? Yes, I believe governments will get it together. Will it be in time? What does in time mean? Is there a plan? Yes, I believe there is a plan.

Climate change can also be about our interior climate. Climate has to do with weather, but it also has to do with our prevailing psychological and spiritual state. Exploring the tensions of the world can bring us to our center. We must be willing to give up everything

---

1   Wilber, Ken. *A Brief History of Everything. Shambhala,* 1996. p. 35.

that holds us back.

We must live day-by-day, moment-to-moment. Torturing ourselves about possible future events is not a way to live. At least it's not the way I choose to live. Instead, learn to see the opportunities in challenges. Learn to smile at the synchronicity that is on display because of life's love for you. I gave up my need to have the world live by my standards a few years ago. I am the only one who needs to live by my standards. That has become enough for me. When we live this way, we live with a better climate, no matter how the climate changes.

Significance: Saturn in Libra, worries, doubts, unsureness, challenge, pain and grief, confusion, growth, freedom, hope, drama, emotion, endings and beginnings, focus, rebirth

Lessons: Saturn is a demanding teacher whom we can befriend. The 3 of Intelligence says that hope arises in despair. In giving, we receive; in sorrow, we learn to experience joy.

Practices: Can you see how your inner climate affects the outer climate of your life? Name a few things you can do to help you and those around you right now. Say hello to the nature around you.

Next Step: Be open to your hardest lessons.

Contemplate: All situations are neutral.

Higher Octave: I can live free of the stories of the world.

Affirmation: I am ready for all challenges in my life.

4 of INTELLIGENCE

Peace is a state we all want to attain—
for ourselves, for our loved ones, for the world—
and it means different things to different people and cultures.

Experience: Peace

The word peace reminds me of the word love. They are both universal terms with many subjective meanings, though their deepest meanings are beyond anything we can articulate. A few dictionary definitions refer to peace as a sense of security in a public place or the absence of war. But there is one definition I want to talk about—peace as the absence of mental stress or anxiety.

One time, I was sitting in a quiet restaurant in India when three people came into the restaurant a bit noisily. One of them recognized that the energy in the restaurant changed in their presence. He said to me, "Sorry to disturb peace." I replied to him, "You can't disturb peace, you can only disturb the story of peace."

The story of peace tells us that our peace depends on outside circumstances. This is a shallow, unstable peace. Actions and noises disrupt the story of peace. We can get emotional, reactive, or even angry when the story of peace is unexpectedly interrupted. When it gets stirred, we feel the antithesis of peace.

On the other hand, the idea that you can't disturb peace means that the feelings of peace come from deep within. This peace is not affected by events and noises in the outer world. This peace rides on the connection to all of life, by *knowing* we are not separate from any aspect of this physical plane world—not from people, nature, animals, suffering, or thoughts.

This deeper peace comes from settling into our True nature. It is a place of contentment, without a need for life or other people to conform to any of our needs or expectations. This settling is solid and doesn't waver. Yes, you might get momentarily throttled by the sound of a motorcycle honking behind you, but you come back to peace as soon as the honking passes. In fact, you never actually leave it. The throttling just covers it up for a bit. Like static on a radio, the radio is still playing underneath the static, even if you can't hear it.

It's up to us to learn the difference in the peace that we feel. Learn to be sensitive to what goes on inside you. Start by experiencing peace while watching the sunset, sitting by the ocean, or walking through a forest. Notice when that peace leaves and learn to settle back into it. Sink into the hug of gravity. This takes a while, so go step by step. Don't expect life to change to meet your requirements. When we are connected, this is peace.

The world is crazy right now. I will not give up my sense of peace for anything. Let the world blow up, if that is what needs to happen. I do not see a need to buy into the tension. This is the resolve we need to attain and maintain for deep peace far beyond the dictionary definitions and common understandings.

Significance: Jupiter in Libra, integration, expansion, contemplation, rest, balance, aggression, stress, revolution, avarice, arrogance, calm, inner unification, meditation

Lessons: The gains we make in life take effort and are worthy of reflection. The 4 of Intelligence reminds us to bask in the fullness of this moment in time. In peace, we feel joy and balance.

Practices: Have you experienced a deep sense of peace? What aspects of your life rob you of peace? Think of ways you can bring more peace into your life.

Next Step: Slow down and appreciate as much as you can.

Contemplate: Live from a calm space.

Higher Octave: Live in peace, not the story of peace.

Affirmation: Inner peace is my birthright.

5 of INTELLIGENCE

The Funky Fish Café and Bar, situated in a small, hip, coastal community in New Zealand, was right out of the 1960s—even its funky restroom. I noticed this place on a walk earlier in the day and made a point to check it out. I had a lovely fish dinner in a very sweet environment with good company, ending a truly perfect day.

Experience: The Bucket Experience

There are lots of different ideas surrounding bucket list experiences across modern culture. The general idea is to avoid regret by satisfying a wish list of things you want to do before you "kick the bucket."

Regret can become a stew of despair. Why do so many of us put off or delay our greatest wishes? Part of the reason may be a lack of money, time, or resources. Or maybe it's because of an abundance of conditioning and personal fears. Sometimes we don't feel like we deserve nice things. Or maybe it never feels like the right time.

These last twenty-five years, I've been able to live like I was checking off a bucket list. I didn't have a plan to do so. Instead, this lifestyle kind of found me. I walked in Genghis Khan's footsteps in Mongolia. I saw incredible sites in China. I explored and bought items in amazing marketplaces all over the world to sell in the U.S. I traveled where I felt to go, finding treasures and having deep experiences along the way.

Regret isn't something I experience. In fact, the closest thing to an item on my own bucket list is completing this book for you to read. Instead of regret, I tend to have the ability to be completely in my experiences. I follow my heart in the moment and am completely full and present. Sometimes when I leave a place, I say only the body leaves. My being is still in the experiences, having rich moments without doubt or regret.

However, many years ago, I had an extraordinary experience with a twist to the bucket list theme.

On my way back from Australia, I spent about a week with a rental car traveling around the North Island of New Zealand. I remember being impressed by the million shades of green in the amazing landscape. From oceans to ancient trees, from folky towns to delicious food, I traveled that week feeling an increasing sense of wholeness and completeness. Toward the end of the week, on the west side of the island, as I headed south to complete my three-hundred-mile circle, I had an experience unlike any I'd had before.

I was on a walk near the ocean before dinner. During the walk, I found a little bench on a tall hillside overlooking the Sun setting behind the ocean. The view was spectacular, the weather perfect, and I had the feeling: *I don't need to move from this spot. If I die right here, right now, I will feel full and complete. I don't need to do anything else in this life.* What I experienced in that moment was the feeling of enough, one of my personal challenges.

The Sun set, the moment passed, I moved on, and went to dinner at the restaurant I mentioned above.

I've had this kind of experience a few times since—moments of complete satiation. This is how I suggest we experience our bucket list moments. When we search for experiences—

bucket list or not— we're really searching for ourselves. We can find ourselves in the experiences. Let's use each moment to practice our eventual physical death by leaving nothing undone in our time here.

Significance: Venus in Aquarius, possible failure and loss, truth, difficulties, one-upmanship, getting something wanted, fear, losing control, objectivity, clarity, freedom, overcoming

Lessons: We all experience moments of regret, despair, and failure. The 5 of Intelligence suggests that all experiences offer an opportunity to improve our attitudes. Just like making lemonade out of lemons, we can see life more clearly when we let go of fears, doubts, and expectations.

Practices: Are you totally in the experiences you have? If not, where are you? Learn to feel peace around things you regret. Bring gratitude to the greatest tests of life.

Next Step: Let go of the ideas of fault and defeat.

Contemplate: Control is an illusion.

Higher Octave: Be and not do.

Affirmation: I am present and open to life.

6 of INTELLIGENCE

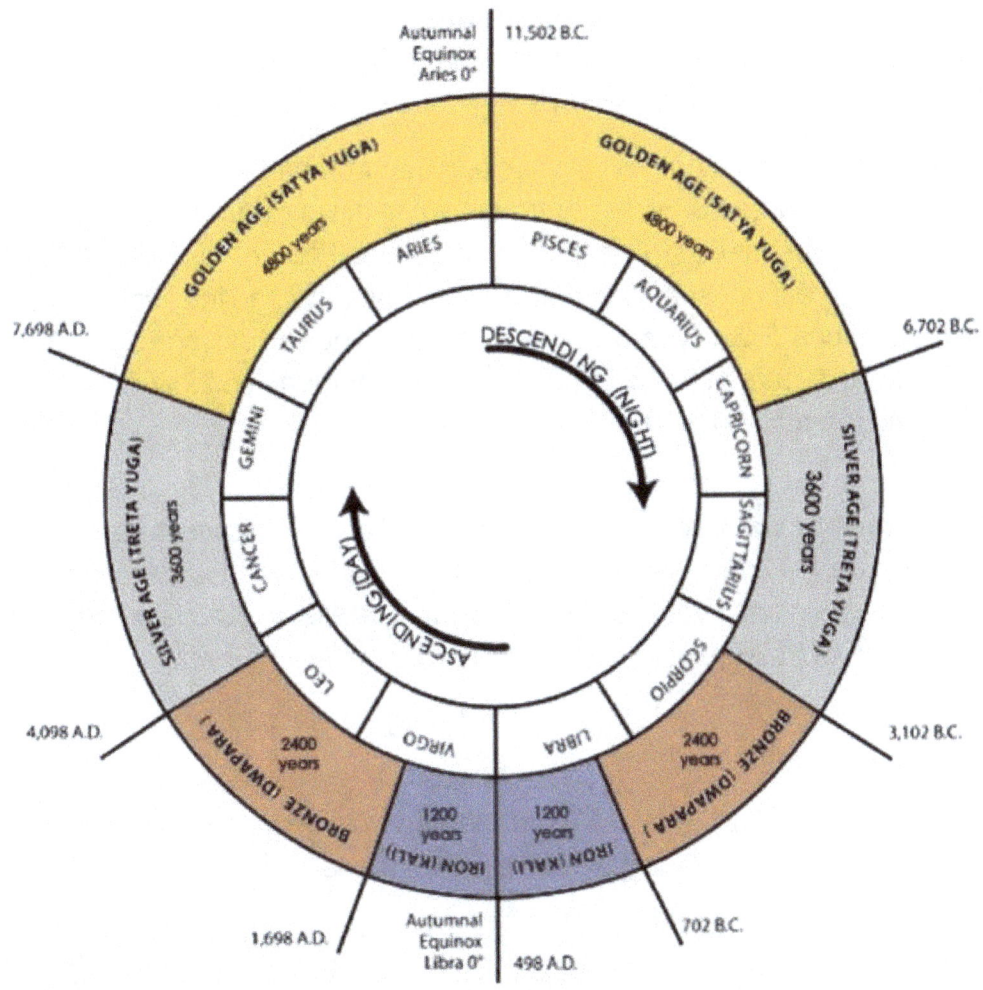

"East and West must establish a golden middle path of activity and spirituality combined… the vibrations there of many spiritually seeking souls come flood like to me. I perceive potential saints in America and Europe, waiting to be awakened."[1]

These words are said to have been spoken by Babaji (Ace of Energy) in January 1894 at the Kumbha Mela in Allahabad, India, and started a domino of events that have touched many awakening souls.

1   Yogananda, Paramahansa. *Autobiography of a Yogi. Crystal Clarity Publishers*, 1946. p. 326.

Experience: The Yugas

A cycle of ages is known to many cultures all over the world. In Greece, the ages are called the Great Year. It is comprised of a Golden Age, Silver Age, Bronze Age, and Iron Age. In India, it is called the Yugas and is an important component of Yogic science. The Yugas are four ages that comprise our cycles of history. The highest age is called Satya Yuga. Second is Treta Yuga. Third is Dwapara Yuga. Last is the densest time, Kali Yuga.

In Satya Yuga, the highest age, human intellect can comprehend all. This period is said to last for 4,000 years with 800 years of transition. In Treta Yuga, the human intellect can comprehend divine magnetism—the source of all electrical forces. This period is 3,000 years long with 600 years of transition. In Dwapara Yuga, human intellect can comprehend fine matters and runs 2,000 years plus 400 years. The lowest age is Kali Yuga,1,000 years long, plus 200 years of transition, during which human intellect cannot comprehend anything beyond the material level of the external world.

This information is based on the work of the well-respected Sri Yukteswar, guru to Paramahansa Yogananda, who authored the spiritual classic, *Autobiography of a Yogi*. Sri Yukteswar gives us the exact dates of these cycles and says that the cycles run in both descending and ascending patterns. The cycle runs parallel to, and is probably influenced by, the Procession of the Equinox.

From 11502 BC to 500 AD, civilization went through a descending cycle, during which information and knowledge were lost.

In 500 AD, at the height of the Dark Ages, the ascending cycle began and will run until 12000 AD. Then, the descending cycle will start all over again.

While all of India thinks we are still in Kali Yuga, Yukteswar claimed that we are in Dwapara Yuga. No one else specifies this dating, and it is not surprising that there is no agreement about which cycle we are in now. There is no decisive way to know. However, many cultures express a strong feeling that we are either in or are soon to enter a higher age. We all feel it.

Descending and Ascending Kali Yuga, from 700 BC to 1700 AD, were known for a matter-driven level of awareness. It had the lowest amount of Dharmic light, meaning that the lower base attitudes of man—greed, war, and lack of respect for life—reigned. It was a dense time, during which life was to be passively endured.

Advancing from there, Dwapara Yuga is known as the Energy Age. We will learn that things are made up of energy. There'll be an expansion of light and new conscious ways of being with and treating each other. Humankind will see through material ways of living, and the mind/body connections become universally respected, advancing society in all ways.

People think we are still in Kali Yuga because some of the gross forms of Kali Yuga are still prevalent around the world. But they are dying, not thriving. In the last century, we saw atomic power, the internet, quantum physics, physiology, huge population explosions, and a revival of 3000-year-old healing modalities, including yoga, tai chi, and acupressure, becoming popular all over the world. The energy is changing, and we can all feel a difference.[1]

Our children and their children will benefit from this undeniable expansion of consciousness. Yes, much work needs to be done to rid ourselves of lower attitudes and vibrations. This process can be downright ugly, and many suffer because of the ignorance and evil of a few. But we are in this together. Our job is to release what does not serve us. When each of us does our small part, we will produce revolutionary changes.

---

1 The book, *The Yugas: Keys to Understanding Our Hidden Past, Emerging Present and Future Enlightenment* by David Steinmetz and Joseph Selbie was used in much of the research and understanding about the Yugas used for this theme.

Significance: Mercury in Aquarius, cosmic changes, science, patience, stuck in time, travel, clarity, stagnation, confusion, analytical skills, deflection, impermanence, new cycle

Lessons: Internal growth spurts are supported by our ability to intellectually perceive the world around us. The 6 of Intelligence shares visions on many levels and perspectives. The wise one learns to trust the process of natural evolution, going with the flow.

Practices: What changes in society's expansion of consciousness have you noticed in your lifetime? Reflect on ways you have changed in your lifetime. Reflect on your gratitude for the world as it is.

Next Step: See your life as your neighbor does.

Contemplate: Impermanence means that everything changes.

Higher Octave: Live life in harmony with nature.

Affirmation: I awake to meet each day with innocence and assurance.

7 of INTELLIGENCE

In studying biological items like genes, cells, and organs, we see a natural evolution from species to species. In the miracle that is the human body, we, the inhabitants, don't make the heart beat or digest the food, but we do help the body perform and evolve by caring for it.

Experience: Modern Christmas Ode

The acceleration of evolutionary growth took about fifty million years to develop, more than five hundred million years ago. Considering the total life span of Earth is four billion years, fifty million years is a small section of time.

Evolution's trial and error resulted in many generations of mutations. Some species worked, and many did not. When nature became a more stable and permissive environment, and resources became more plentiful, larger animals and humans appeared. Humans are the most complex system of animals, and they developed fairly recently.

The human body contains wisdom that can help the being that exists within it. This is the gift we are given at birth. Sing out like it's a modern Christmas ode to the sanctity of human life. The body evolved through natural means for millions of years and is made conscious by the soul that enters it. All life is conscious.

Sri Yukteswar said, "Man's body is precious. It has the highest evolutionary value because of unique brain and spinal centers. These enable the advanced devotee to fully grasp and express the loftiest aspects of divinity. No lower form is so equipped."[1]

The body is very pure. It is able to give us perceptions separate from any human or mental bias. It's pure biology, which works as a mirror to consciousness.

As such, the body is another vehicle through which we can understand life, ourselves, and our true nature. It provides a clarity that is not so obvious in the everyday world. Even if the outside world is a dream, it does seem to flow, project, and exist in predictable ways. That predictability contains wisdom.

There is beauty and perfection in our having a human vehicle for Essence to enter. The ego, whatever it is and if it exists, wants us to believe that we are the body—to tie us down to mind and thought.

Biological life and soul life live in parallel worlds that manifest according to their own perfect laws. We can only change the Universe by changing ourselves. Like water taking different shapes, the Universe can change form as we transform ourselves inside and out.

We all have different functions, viewpoints, skills, and focuses to add to the collective pot. Together, we are a whole. One does not have to adapt to all the points of view for survival. Each of us has a uniqueness, just as there are different varieties of birds and breeds of dogs. When we focus on our individual highest octaves, we can naturally flow to our highest purposes, embodying universal peace and awakening unto our *true self.*

---

1   Yogananda, Paramahansa. *Autobiography of a Yogi. Crystal Clarity Publishers*, 1946. p. 112.

Significance: Moon in Aquarius, being our own worst enemy, friendship, self-awareness, deceit, contradictions, duality, personal growth, diminishment, sensitivity, unconscious

Lessons: As evolution is ongoing, we cycle from high highs to low lows. The 7 of Intelligence wants to help us create circumstances in which we can consciously succeed. Fears and doubts can be springboards for greater understanding and confidence.

Practices: Meditate on the miracle of a human body. Can you name some bodily functions that happen automatically, without any input from us? Mediate on the Earth as seen from space. Think about all that happens on the surface.

Next Step: Love the self.

Contemplate: Recognize and have gratitude for the miracle of this life.

Higher Octave: Live life for others and Self.

Affirmation: I am the master of my life.

8 of INTELLIGENCE

A warm kitty purring in a lap feels complete in the moment, producing feelings in us of arrival, settlement, and love— of being home and belonging.

Experience: Remembrance

We all have experiences like these. Our mate is on a long business trip, a friend receives unsettling news from the doctor, or maybe our cat is uncharacteristically out for the whole night. While we wait for an arrival or news, we are unsettled. Then, when we are finally reunited with those we've missed, we feel relaxed and relieved. We are settled once again.

The tensions we feel in these kinds of unknowing minutes have many physical effects on us. It can be hard on our body in the long term as we live from tension to tension. Digestion is slowed. We lose sleep. Joints become stiff. We develop physical aches. We live in the invented mental stories, fantasizing realities that mostly never come true. Plans get put on hold as a certain paralysis occurs. In these tensions, we are not living in the moment. However, the purpose of these experiences can be to teach us not to live this way anymore.

As a counterpoint to the effects of worry and pain inherent in life, other experiences are capable of fostering relaxation. When I first visited India in 1986, the whole trip was characterized by remembrance. This remembrance was not about specific memories of places or experiences. It was a feeling of coming home—maybe to India, but also to a place within me. I walked around with a deep smile on my face and with a deep sense of peace that had me floating. I didn't really understand the depth of my experience back then, but I did identify a gap when I was back in the U.S. There was a space between my "normal" consciousness and the depth of consciousness that I had experienced in India. I spent a long time trying to understand and fill that gap.

Remembrance, in my experience, is a feeling of belonging. It is not about specific memories. It is a *knowing*—a feeling of being in the right place, and of completeness. We know that whatever we're experiencing is "right" for us, almost like time stands still. These feelings appear viscerally within the body. I feel them as depth and stillness. The feelings may be new to the mind, but they are not new to the ancient all-knowing Self inside us.

Beyond the feeling of remembrance, we also embody the energy of remembrance. We are relaxation itself. When we put our effort into living with this reality, miracles seem to appear.

At one point while writing this book, I experienced some computer difficulty—the blue screen of death. And although I have to admit that I was a little worried, I remembered to stay connected to feelings of protection and guidance. I chose to tap into the *knowing* that if I were to lose this book all would still be okay. I was not willing to give up that sense of peace. Then, inexplicably and only hours later, my computer seemed happy and started up again like nothing had happened before. A miracle. And a reminder from the guru called Life that moments of difficulty do not have to take our peace.

When we live life in a soft remembrance, relaxed, like sitting on the beach without a care in the world, even during tough moments, peace is always waiting for us.

Significance: Jupiter in Gemini, recognition, indecision, fear, self-limiting, freedom, blinded, giving away power, imprisonment, clarity, brain fog, doubt, returning confidence, resolution

Lessons: Life can be filled with moments of pain, doubts, and suffering. The 8 of Intelligence suggests that we release them by coming back to our warm, fuzzy *self*. Like the caged bird that flies away when presented with an opportunity, releasing our interferences will bring clarity and movement.

Practices: Have you had the remembrance experience? See if you can bring a feeling of remembrance to a difficult situation in your life. Love whatever comes your way.

Next Step: Be free and clear in the next moment.

Contemplate: Let things be as they are. Solutions come when we stop trying.

Higher Octave: I am guided and protected.

Affirmation: I trust in the perfection of each moment.

9 of INTELLIGENCE

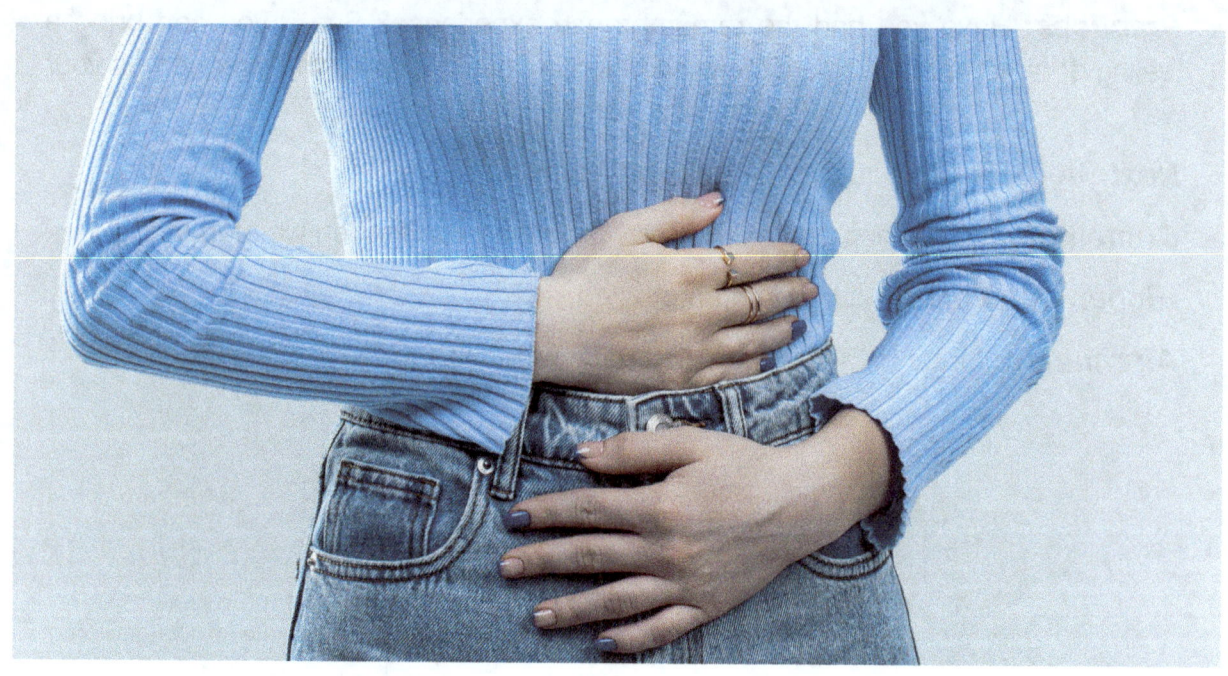

It is easy to get stuck in the head—the home of our mental faculties. But it's in our stomach and gut that a lot of important work occurs. Intuition, digestion, and peace all start there.

Experience: Feeding the Body

Why do we need to waste so much time, money, and energy on eating three times a day? We buy food, cook it, eat it, clean up the mess, and eliminate it from our body, day after day, for an entire lifetime. Surely this was bad planning by the supreme planner.

However, when we study this issue from a scientific viewpoint, eating provides nourishment to sustain bodily systems and functions. All organisms, down to a single cell, need some form of food to sustain life. And let's face it: Many animals spend most of their days simply trying to acquire food. It is their most basic and important function. Animals don't get vacations or weekends. They can't buy food at grocery stores or restaurants.

When we move forward in thinking from eating to digestion, it is simply miraculous how digestion happens on its own. But for many of us, digestion has become a problem. The internet says that an astounding 74 percent of people experience GI discomfort. That's a lot of people!

From digestive discomfort comes mental suffering, consumption of Western medicines, and loss of sleep. If our digestive systems aren't working as they should, we experience a net loss of energy from food consumption instead of a net gain.

Is there a deeper purpose to this whole process?

Looking at life from a spiritual viewpoint, we are spiritual beings living a human experience in human bodies. Is the purpose to be able to drink wine and eat a fine meal in a nice restaurant with friends? I don't think that is the purpose, but that is something we can enjoy.

The purpose, instead, could be to learn lessons that we cannot learn anywhere else. Is there something that eating teaches us? I began to consider feeding the body three times a day as a holy act. These mundane human acts ground us into sacred *mudras*— physical motions—of maintaining the care of our bodily temple. They can be perceived as ceremonial—a way to honor our miraculous, sacred frame. Trillions of cells united, each with its own singular function, to provide a living environment for the Self.

Something as simple as a meal teaches us to slow down and encourages us to come to our center. The meal itself becomes a path on which we can explore our own nature. What a blessing it is to have a body that needs to be cared for. Like we do with anything that we love in this world, let's remember to treat it well, and feel love while feeding the body

Significance: Mars in Gemini, anxiety, guilt, patience, understanding, despair, shame, hurting oneself, recognition, overcoming, relaxation, strength, necessity, assurance, trust, freedom

Lessons: The 9 of Intelligence suggests that we look beyond pain to see the miracles of life. Mundane acts are anything but mundane when we remember how sacred and holy life is.

Practices: Think about where your food came from and how it arrived to you as your meal. Visualize the food you eat as it makes its way through your body. Bring a moment of acknowledgement or prayer to the beginning of each meal.

Next Step: Whenever you notice yourself spiraling, come to a place of neutrality and peace.

Contemplate: Stop judging and start forgiving.

Higher Octave: Love yourself as you are. Then love everyone else as they are.

Affirmation: I have everything I need to be the best *self*.

10 of INTELLIGENCE

There is a public restroom in a park in Tokyo, Japan, created by a prize-winning architect, that has smart glass that stays transparent when the restroom is empty and becomes opaque when occupied. The glass allows occupants to feel safe knowing the public restroom is empty before use and private and secure when using.

Experience: Are We Safe in Safety?

I've been intrigued lately by the word "safe" or "safety." It has been appearing in my healing journey and in my readings. I see it used in various ways, such as "It is not safe for me..." "I can only be safe when..." "XYZ keeps me safe."

Perhaps everything we do has a goal of safety. After all, our biological nature is to protect ourselves from harm, danger, and the unknown. But what is safe in this world? Why do we think that certain situations are safe or not safe? How do we overcome fears of the unknown? How can we secure safety? I don't have the answers, but I bring these questions up to initiate further inward discussions.

Let's start with a definition of safety. Safety is "the state of being certain that adverse effects will not be caused by some agent under defined conditions."[1] Depending on your defined conditions, is it safe in safety? Is safety an oxymoron? There are always dangers to the physical form. We are always subject to adverse effects and challenges. There is no safe place to hide without some agent.

However, the idea of safety that I want to focus on is usually based on protecting our ego and mind. *It is not safe means: I will have to surrender and give up positions I hold. I will lose the safety of living in separation. I will live so that I don't let parts of life come close to me, thus avoiding feeling my pains.*

When we develop trust, we realize that we are not in control of anything. There is a cosmic intelligence to the experience of life. The heart beats, the food digests, the Sun rises—these happen from a power outside our human form, though we are it too. When we live from this Truth, we trust and always feel safe.

Feeling safe allows the self to be open and vulnerable and can be one of the last fears to overcome on any spiritual journey. Trusting that what we need is already available can help transcend the need.

The knowledge that our heart beats on its own is what keeps us safe because we are trusting. We recognize God as universality. This universality *is* us and within us. The more that we accept and become comfortable with that, the more our trust increases. There is something greater than this material world that is constantly supporting us. That is the safe in safety.

---

1   This particular definition came from WordWeb, a free online Dictionary and Thesaurus downloaded as an app on the Author's computer.

Significance: Sun and Moon in Gemini, destruction, disaster, desolation, loss and separation, insanity, paranoia, hope, prayer, alignment, trust, faith, security, challenges, resolution

Lessons: There are times, long and short, when things seem like they're not going to work out. The 10 of Intelligence shares that focusing on the higher Truths can help bridge any height. Situations change with time and effort, just as the dark of night becomes the light of day.

Practices: Breathe deeply through the intellectual understanding that we don't need protection because we are already protected. Recognize your fears and begin to release them.

Next Step: Develop objectivity about subjective experiences.

Contemplate: I am always safe.

Higher Octave: Be open and vulnerable to accept what is.

Affirmation: I trust that I am safe and protected.

ACE of GRAVITY

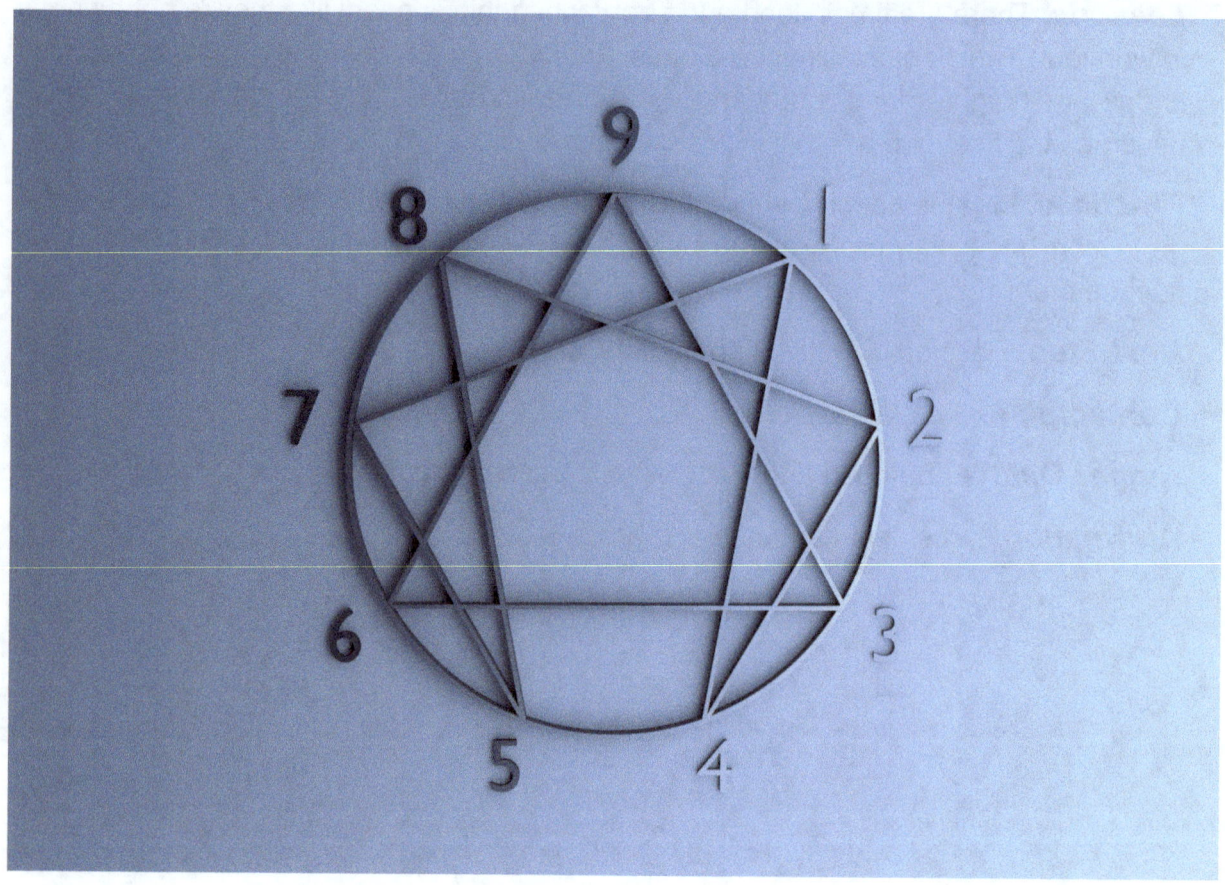

The figure representing the Enneagram of Personality is composed of three geometric shapes that combine to form nine points or personality styles. The three shapes are a circle, which represents the unity of the whole; a triangle, representing the Law of Three; and a hexad, a six-sided figure that represents the Law of Seven.

The Law of Three says that every action contains three interacting forces— the active, the passive, and the reconciliating. The Law of Seven states that everything changes. These are fundamental laws concerning the nature of the Universe. G.I. Gurdjieff, who introduced us to the Enneagram form over one hundred years ago, believed that all the knowledge of the Universe can be read within the Enneagram.

Experience: The Enneagram of Personality

The Enneagram of Personality is a tool for understanding and reducing the hold of the human psyche that emerged in the 1960s. Our understanding of it continues to expand and evolve. The word Enneagram comes from a Greek word that means "nine-sided figure." It is a system of study that believes there are nine personality styles or points. These personality styles explain the patterned ways in which we interact with the world. We are each born with one of the styles at our core. Why nine? We are a social species, we need the nine personalities. If we all had the same personality, not much would get done.

The Enneagram is a wonderful psychological tool that gives us a comprehensive understanding of our core triggers and the strategies the mind and ego use to protect ourselves from the cultural conditioning and compulsions that drive us. Working with the Enneagram helps us to learn to release and dissolve 5,000 years of Judeo-Christian tradition—the conditioning passed down from generation to generation. It also helps us have more compassionate relationships with ourselves and others.

As a map for spiritual growth, the Enneagram is unique. It has the ability to clearly define our core fears, angers, and emotions, and what keeps us attached to them. No other teacher or system so accurately highlights, without bias, our unique paths toward the home Essence. By recognizing our innate patterning, we can release triggers and delve into core behavior. Observing our behavior loosens the ego's hold, allowing us to become more aware. From that awareness, we can choose new behavior rather than the old patterned behavior.

I've been working toward my own growth and understanding with the Enneagram of Personality since the late 1990s, and now I share it through teaching and readings. The insights are never-ending. While the patterns box us in, freedom lies in the knowledge and understanding of those patterns. As a map for finding the inner center, Enneagram is unparalleled, deepening inner peace and wisdom.

With that freedom, we can naturally develop and share our unique gifts and skills.

There is a test to find your Enneagram number at http://indrarinzler.com/enneagram-tests

Significance: Knowledge, patience, success, wholeness, confidence, frustration, restriction, fragmentation, inner awareness, personal prosperity, growth, contentment

Lessons: Prosperity and inner peace are universal life goals. The Ace of Gravity shares that we can learn how to get out of our own way and realize our goals.

Practices: Observe the ways in which your personality and behaviors change when you are stressed or relaxed. Can you feel your core triggers? How would your life change if you were completely content?

Next Step: Notice your own behaviors without judgment.

Contemplate: Body and soul can meet in harmonious union.

Higher Octave: I am free of all stories that weigh me down.

Affirmation: Freedom from my limiting beliefs opens me to the whole Universe.

2 of GRAVITY

The nature of duality exists within our Universe as yin and yang, good and bad, light and dark, up and down. Duality teaches us that by being exposed to polar extremes, we are encouraged toward the center of our being. Assimilating both sides is unity.

Experience: The Polarity of Relationship

Part of the complexity of human relations is that we tend to polarize each other by assuming others maintain contradictory tendencies, perspectives, and beliefs from our own. Polarity is a real force in nature. However, complementary forces work together to create balance. Where duality divides things into black or white, polarity includes the full spectrum.

For example, let's look at parenting styles in Joe and Sally. Sally tends to be stricter, while Joe tends toward leniency. Over time, it's hard for Sally to be seen as a lenient parent because Joe will always seem more lenient. Thus, as with many couples, Sally feels she needs to be stricter to balance Joe out.

These kinds of situations in life can lead to blame and arguments. We fight to be seen as the right one, even though nobody is ultimately right or wrong.

This doesn't just happen in relationships. We disagree with neighbors, food servers, and traffic lights. Political and religious discussions quickly become polarized. When life doesn't go the way we want, we react with self-righteousness. Life has a way of putting these situations in front of us to teach us the need for balance.

The way out of these dilemmas is not easy. It takes maturity, compassion, and communication skills. Offering grace and being honest about our feelings can offer a sense of resolution. If we want a way out of polarization, we can open our minds to creative choices outside the duality of two. We can live on a higher level.

Let go of the limitation of absolutes. Be willing to let yourself outside of the positions you hold. Balance helps us come to center. Little by little, we find the center and release polarizing positions in all the relationships in life.

Significance: Jupiter in Capricorn, fluctuation, agitation, change, balance, priorities, flexibility, adaptability, adjustment, impossibility, restriction, enrichment, expansion

Lessons: Life continually tests our ability to find confidence in balance. The 2 of Gravity suggests that natural forces at work teach us to rise above them. Change is out of our hands. We can learn to flow with the gravity of each situation.

Practices: Do you live up to your ideals? Do you live with inconsistencies? What qualities do you admire in others? Where do you feel weak? Reflect on your inner work and how much you've grown and changed throughout your life.

Next Step: It's okay to be misunderstood and misheard.

Contemplate: We are all One.

Higher Octave: Support the highest in others.

Affirmation: I affirm all points of view as possible.

3 of GRAVITY

The ripples created by the mind, ripple outside us, but also ripple inside us. We may try to numb ourselves to our own experiences by turning to stone, but the ripples impact us anyway.

Experience: Mind/Body

There is a close relationship between the mind and the body. I believe the two are physically and psychically intertwined. Tending to both will heal many modern ailments.

Many times, we try to heal illness by attacking the symptoms. However, symptoms do not speak to root causes. Medicine can remove symptoms, but it can also create others or even infect other parts of the body. Or, maybe, we continue to re-infect ourselves with our mind.

For example, let's examine Jane. Jane grows up in a contentious relationship with her single mother. As she gets older, she learns to hate herself and her life. Then, in her early twenties, she begins experiencing digestion problems, backaches, and a series of bad relationships. When she goes to the doctor to address a flare-up of symptoms after a bad breakup, she is prescribed medication that treats some of her surface-level symptoms. Although it brings some relief, Jane's body remains in a cycle of progress and then discomfort.

Jane lives like this for decades until she is introduced to alternative healing. After learning more, she begins looking closely at her life. She wonders if, instead of a medical condition, a combination of her own choices and bad karma is the cause of her despair.

Then, one day, Jane learns that holding onto mental resentment towards others and oneself can cause chemical reactions in the body, inhibiting digestion and causing pain.

So, Jane takes a two-week vacation and starts the process of truly healing. She allows her body to relax. She starts learning to love herself. She forgives her mother and all her ex-boyfriends. She finds gratitude for the life she lives and how far she has come. She begins to feel lighter, and her digestion improves.

There are times when harsh feelings flare up again. She gets a call from her mother. An ex-boyfriend reaches out on social media. But when she can come back to center after being unexpectedly thrown off, her symptoms and ailments all but disappear.

All types of pains and ailments in our bodies can teach us about troubles in our minds. Joint pain can signal inflexibility; heart disease can come from a closed heart; eye trouble can be an inability to see other points of view; and ear problems can signal a lack of close listening.

The body was developed over millions of years. The mind is a miraculous tool. We have no idea what the mind/body really is, but it contains wisdom that we can learn to respect. It is sensitive and brilliant beyond our understanding and maybe even our imagination. It could be that the whole point of life is to wake up to our real nature—to see that the body and mind are not who we are. But they do provide us with a temple within which we reside.

Take care of that temple, my friends, and mind/body will take care of you.

Significance: Mars in Capricorn, self-mastery, excellence, full effort, expansion, affirmation, collaboration, focus, obligation, spirit, distraction, no passion, mediocrity, progress

Lessons: We never stop learning and growing through challenges in life. The 3 of Gravity offers practicality as a step in our process. Tuning into the body and mind is like using a compass to help find our way.

Practices: Have you experienced how your thoughts can affect your body? Do external events create tension in your body? What would it feel like to let go of stress and be free?

Next Step: Full recovery takes place in all aspects of the being.

Contemplate: Body and mind work in harmony.

Higher Octave: Release body tensions and the thoughts that cause them.

Affirmation: I am well and whole, and able to meet any challenge.

4 of GRAVITY

*The Sun provides all the light, heat, and life in our solar system.
99.86 percent of the solar system's mass comes from the Sun.
An astounding 4.6 billion years old and 93 million miles from Earth,
it's large enough to be able to fit one million Earths inside. The Sun is
27 million degrees at its center and a mere one million degrees at the
surface. In astrology, the Sun represents the self, will, self-esteem,
pride, and sense of purpose.*

Experience: What is Astrology?

Astrology is the study of the influence of constellations and planets on human lives. An astrology chart is a map of the solar system at the time we are born. According to their training, skill, and intuition, astrologers read the chart to make determinations about our life.

The planets imprint us at birth with electromagnetic energy based on their placement. We inherit the highs and lows of this energy and compensate for the feelings they cause through our behaviors. Astrology's archetypes are human-derived. Planets act as our celestial parents by manifesting the neutral energy behind the archetypes. One of astrology's oldest sayings is, "The stars incline, but don't compel."

Astrology reflects real forces at work. It's an astral weather map helping us to navigate life. However, we don't need to feel limited by our charts. Life encourages us to live beyond our conditioning. The highest use of astrology supports our waking to the present moment by learning to see through the celestial conditions.

Astrology is the mother of all sciences and used to be the same as what is now called astronomy. The concept of time developed from observing the planets, and days of the week were named after the planets. Furthermore, many organisms have developed internal clocks and calendars that are basic to their survival. These clocks are affected by seasonal changes in light, gravitational energy, and the Earth's magnetic field. Bees and birds navigate by the Sun and night sky. The entire solar system affects Earth's weather and climate patterns.

Some say astrology is a pseudoscience because it does not always pass the tests of the scientific method. We can't measure astrology with a ruler. We can't put it on a scale or in a centrifuge. However, science changes when the facts change. New ideas become known, and then they become the latest science. I expect a golden age ahead in which the scientific and energetic truths of astrology will be understood and accepted.

Astrology has mathematical roots and is based on the constant cycles and patterns found in nature. It is a practice of blending science and intuitive art. It shines light on our natural strengths and weaknesses.

By understanding the planetary alignment at our birth, we can be more objective about our behavior and challenges in life. Life, like the tides, has ebbs and flows. When we can live on a grand scale, we can row *with* our challenges and not against them. This is the highest gift astrology offers us.

Significance: Sun in Capricorn, power, control, rigidity, distrust, security, self-knowledge, gift, inheritance, self-awareness, finding equanimity, paralysis, impotency, self-centered

Lessons: It is difficult to be stable and assured with the challenges of modern life. The 4 of Gravity offers the power inherent in true celestial knowledge. It is the nature of Truth to keep us centered and at a distance from the extremes of self-centeredness and rigid, distrustful behavior.

Practices: Have you discovered any patterns within yourself during daily ups and downs? Have you felt affected by events outside yourself? Have you noticed times of the year when you are always happy or sad?

Next Step: Get your head out of the clouds.

Contemplate: The patterned nature of behavior.

Higher Octave: I live according to my true nature.

Affirmation: I shine during every moment of my life.

5 of GRAVITY

*Over time, we play many roles on the stage of life.
I've come to realize that the enlightened ones get off the stage
and learn to observe the play from the audience. This enables
greater clarity and releases the residue of any roles we played.*

Experience: Messages to Younger Selves

Many of us are not so good at listening to and utilizing advice from other people, especially when we are young and stubborn. We know we need to eat better and exercise more, but we can be resistant to lifestyle and personal changes of all kinds for a long time. Somehow, it's even harder for us to listen when someone tells us something directly.

The wisdom of elders isn't really respected in our modern society. Roles have changed over time. How can we find the balance to be able to move forward in the ways we grow, and yet hold back when that is appropriate? This life is a beautiful dance. We come here to grow. We use the knowledge stored in our DNA. We understand so little about evolution. But we don't have to understand something to gain value from it. We are so blessed.

At any age, we might tend towards certain perspectives, behaviors, and growth potential. When we understand where and how we fit into the maturation cycles—the stage we are in and on—we add wisdom and clarity to our search for happiness.

In our teens, we are open and malleable. We can quickly change, but are often limited by age, lack of independence, and the viewpoints and beliefs of our family and friends.

In our early twenties, we are open but do not understand enough of what we don't understand. We are more excited by the ability to drive our own life and make our own decisions.

The mid-twenties is a perfect age. We are open and pliable, yet have enough experience to understand problems and solutions. We can be idealistic, but not so self-defined by what we do.

In our late twenties, we start to get a little rigid. Changes come slower. We start to believe our own nonsense.

In our thirties, we become more set in our ways and begin to question the choices that we made in our twenties. We allow ourselves to identify with our thoughts and judgments of right and wrong. This time can be the peak of arrogance and a feeling that we know best.

In our forties, the body isn't what it used to be, we are bogged down by responsibility, and we may start to experience a lot of major changes in relationships, career, living situations, and more. We want to enjoy life, and although we are still somewhat self-defined, we are willing to give up what we know to grow and change. There is a sense that there must be more to life. Perspectives start to change and a new feeling of optimism can take hold.

In our fifties, a new energy appears. As responsibilities to family and career begin to slow, a responsibility for *self* takes over. Hormones, ego, and identity have died down. This can be like a rebirth with an ability to explore blind spots and vulnerabilities. We stop taking everything so seriously. The openness of the twenties may reappear and with it some old interests, with new resolve. We allow the flow of life to start taking hold. Synchronicity happens more often. Do we dare? Absolutely!

In our sixties, the body may show some wear and tear, but it is time to set the sails. Nothing can stop us now. There is no longer a need to be stiff and guarded. We can release the *shoulds* of life learned from family and society. We can see sunshine every day, even when it's rainy and cloudy. We are no longer willing to be held back by resistance.

In our seventies, we finally learn what we haven't understood before. A feeling of a lack of time gives a sense of freedom. The willingness to release is instant. We no longer worry about looks, status, or social rules. It's okay that there is not much time left. Honesty and kindness lead.

In our eighties, we know that we know nothing. We are like the Buddha—inspirational and childlike, lighthearted and soft. Inner peace is at the forefront, and hopefully, we allow ourselves a sense of freedom around what we have and have not done in life. No regrets should live here. Self-satisfaction is enough.

Regrets can appear at any age for things undone in earlier life. For some, the freedom of the 50's can be the time to attain accomplishments and experiences. You CAN find a sense of freedom. With this freedom comes the wisdom that you know nothing. An inner peace will come. Self-satisfaction is enough. This is an important message to share with the younger self.

Significance: Mercury in Taurus, growth, freedom, increasing communication, listening, shame, blame, faults, insecurity, resistance, breakthrough, feet on ground, hope, knowledge

Lessons: At all stages of life, worry and ruin are a possibility. The 5 of Gravity encourages us to learn from hardships. Health and spiritual progress will unfold as we take advantage of opportunities for communication and honesty.

Practices: Recognize any limitations or resistances you see in yourself. Review your earlier life and accept your actions. Appreciate someone older than you who has qualities you admire.

Next Step: Live honestly and openly.

Contemplate: I am right where I need to be.

Higher Octave: I am always serving humanity.

Affirmation: I am what I am, and that's all that I am.

6 of GRAVITY

We are the rose.
This is enough for a while when we repose.
Then we get brushed against.
We look around and see prettier roses and are tense.
We develop thorns and ways to believe that we are protected.
We develop pride around showing our vulnerability and are infected.
But, in reality, all the thorns are not so effective.
Who wants to hug a thorn and be corrected?
With maturity, we take responsibility for our actions,
Releasing doubts and fears and living in factions.
We feel gratitude for the others in our life,
And can bloom fully, appreciated for beauty, without strife.
Peace comes to visit and isn't forlorn,
To see that, we are the rose and the thorn.

Experience: A Day in the Life

One morning, my friend Kimberly sent me an article about women in India fighting for the ability to safely conduct their daily toilet functions. For thousands of years, women have experienced shame around where and how to go. Indoor toilets and plumbing are not available for untold millions. Since there are cultural concerns over purity in the house, many women go out before dawn and after sunset to eliminate outside without the watchful eyes of jeering men. Farmers don't want them in their fields and chase them with sticks. The women sometimes need to walk long distances through rain, fog, insects, and mud to find their safe place. Sometimes they go in groups for safety from possible attacks and rape.

The article was about one brave woman, who grew up in a city with indoor plumbing, suddenly finding herself married and living with her husband's family in a rural village without indoor plumbing. She attempted to bring indoor toilets to her village by helping to build two hundred and fifty of them in the village.

The general plight of women to find safety in male-dominated societies is something that I, as a man, cannot fully appreciate. It's why I got sent the article.

Later that same morning, I connected with another friend. This friend embraces a sensitivity that inspires me. She asked a question about how her neediness fit into her understanding of her *self*. I could tell she was insecure and a little anxious, and I tried to reassure her that her vulnerability inspired me. She said that the idea of needing made her feel lonely, uncertain, and unprotected. I told her that there is no such thing as wrong or missing. Though we feel the negativity, they don't exist in nature, only in the thinking mind. We are never alone; we just feel alone. Uncertainty is for certain, no need to doubt it or hide from it. She said I was helpful to her.

At lunch, I read from the timeless classic, *The Little Prince.* There is a part about a sheep eating a rose with thorns. I found myself suddenly crying. I had no idea why, but I can guess that a beautiful flower's need for thorns was just too much for that moment. Somehow, the thorns held some power over me that turned me to dust.

What did I know about vulnerability compared to the women of India? How could I comprehend the power of a longing that brings us to despair about our place in existence? Why would a beautiful flower need to have thorns? And if there was a why, how was I to coexist in that world?

After lunch, I had a session with my teacher. I was encouraged to grow by being open and vulnerable. Love myself as I am. Stop using the mind. I felt honored by these simple truths. These I could do. I was supported in this growth, whether I knew it or not. I was told beautiful things would happen, and that the time was getting closer.

I went to kirtan in the evening, where there was a small group of souls singing together in a circle lit by candles. The voices were beautiful. The sounds of the guitar and harmonium filled all the space in the room. While sitting on the floor, I was quiet inside.

A friend stopped by for dinner, and we talked about the news of the day, followed by deeper conversation. As the day wound down, I felt the day's events were tied together. The world gives us two choices: love the fear or fear the love. Which of the two will we choose? To see life through fear keeps us small and doubting. We refuse our rightful place at the table of life. Conversely, love is complete and whole—a simple, deep truth that needs nothing else.

I ended up having trouble sleeping that night. It was late enough for tomorrow to become today before I slept for a few hours. We have not been in a high age in recent human history, man's inhumanity to man. There are greater and more conscious ways to treat and be with each other than we experience most days. I need to have peace with this, too. As a society, a greater age will come, but not in my lifetime. It will be a time when we live for a greater good and all decisions are made collectively. I find contentment with this, just as I am content to do my share, giving thanks on a day in my life.

Significance: Moon in Taurus, emotional stability, balance, investment, success, generosity, exchange, purity, release, envy, illusion, desire, naivety, harmony, profit, maturation, peace

Lessons: Each day is a microcosm of our life, with opportunities to grow and be in balance. The 6 of Gravity shares that challenges can lead to success when we live life with this in mind. Love, serve, remember, and give thanks humbly.

Practices: Can you see a wholeness in your day? Which part of the theme above touches you the deepest? Explore how you choose fear or love in your life.

Next Step: Always start with prayerful gratitude.

Contemplate: The fullness and opportunities of each day.

Higher Octave: Accept what can't be accepted.

Affirmation: I am whole and complete in every moment.

7 of GRAVITY

It's the big game—the defining moment of your life so far. Your fans are quietly praying. The opponent's fans are yelling in protest. All your practice and preparation are in the past. It's just you, the basket, and two ticks on a clock—a test of focus and determination. How will you be in this moment?

Experience: Moment

What's it like being in the moment?

Imagine yourself in high school. Your school is playing its big rival in a basketball game. The game is tied, and in the last two seconds, it comes down to you at the free throw line with a chance to win the game. What are you thinking about? A few minutes after the game, win or lose, you'll have a million thoughts about the outcome. But right in this moment, as you bounce the ball before the shot, your mind, body, and existence have a single-pointed focus. The crowd and your teammates, even your coach, disappear. There is only the ball and the basket.

This is what living in the moment is like. You experience what is right here, right now. No past, no future, no right, no wrong—none of it exists. The moment is full and complete. Nothing is missing—no anxiety, no regrets, no needs, no lack, and no separation. Take a breath and be with that breath. If thoughts come, let them go.

Living in the moment, we simply string these experiences together, moment to moment. We stay in a neutral space no matter what life throws at us. We are in it, but not of it. We care, but not at the cost of leaving our *self*.

Let's go back to that imaginary basketball game. In the Hollywood movie version of that moment, as you bounce the ball and gather focus, the images fade to a flashback. Your father hands you a basketball for the first time at age four. The ball is bigger than your head. Next, you bounce the ball with your father, brother, sister—anyone. As the years pass, your skills improve. The ball makes it into the net more frequently. Then the games start. First, elementary, then junior high school. As you enter high school, you spend hours upon hours practicing, sleeping with the basketball, and playing for fun with friends after school. Watching pro and college games, you play out your own big moment in your imagination. Finally, the scene comes back to the free throw line and your own big moment at this high school game.

We need to play out this same montage in our own lives, but without the camera. A lifetime of high notes and low notes are practice for living in every moment.

As the moments of practice turn into years of practice, we begin to forget about the form needed. We act without thinking, like driving a car or riding a bike. Effort over time leads to effortless action. The goals that drive us disappear as we step to our own free throw line for the big shot. The crowd disappears and we become one with our experiences. We take a deep breath and, *swoosh*—the ball goes in the net.

Significance: Saturn in Taurus, patience, contentment, dissatisfaction, disillusionment, contradictions, fear, follow through, powerful thought-forms, expectations, courage, hope

Lessons: It may seem that success and failure can hinge on a particular moment or event. The 7 of Gravity reminds us that cycles come and go in the unfolding of our being. Holding expectations about the past or the future will leave us with dissatisfaction in the moment.

Practices: At your core, what is the game you want to win? How do you practice, day to day, moment to moment? What do you imagine you would miss while living in the moment?

Next Step: Do nothing completely.

Contemplate: The impossible is possible.

Higher Octave: Everything that happens serves the highest good.

Affirmation: I adopt positive attitudes that replace fear.

8 of GRAVITY

*The quiet space of high-altitude vibrations is life-changing.
This rarefied air is available everywhere on Earth by attuning
ourselves to this level of empty high-frequency vibration. Seclusion is
one way to get there. The more you do, the deeper you go.
The reward is inner greatness.*

Experience: Seclusion, the Price of Greatness

During my years living in a spiritual community, I heard a phase repeated many times: seclusion is the price of greatness. Seclusion is a time of contemplation and introspection during which one spends time alone in nature. Those of us who worked community jobs were given one week a year during which we could go into seclusion and dive deep into our spiritual practices, which included time for study and being in nature.

I mediated six to seven hours a day in seclusion. I would not say that this was deep, restless-free meditation, but it was interesting that, year to year, I was able to start where I ended meditatively the year before. I was able to connect to an inner self, different from the everyday outer self. This inner self was more open and vulnerable. As I look back on those times, they did help mold, or at least positively affect, all that has appeared since.

Though I know it would be beneficial for all readers to arrange your lives to experience deep seclusion, it is not something that I expect many of you will, or can, do. Seclusion is not easy. On the physical plane, finding a place and time can be difficult, if not impossible.

Greatness is an inward reward. Greatness is living a life of inward joy and bliss—finding deeper meaning in simple things with assurance and confidence. While this greatness is our birthright, we lose it in this modern world by adopting unhealthy attitudes and insecurities. In fact, we are encouraged to be ordinary and live according to more worldly standards. It can take a long time and many false bottoms before we see through this.

In our busy, modern, media-filled lives, we don't spend enough time in quiet. Quiet means without distractions, and hopefully alone in nature. How much time have you spent alone in nature in the last month? Many people don't even give themselves a quiet time at the end of the day—a reset, a time of reflection, a time to catch our breath. What is the cumulative effect of not doing this? What is the cost? Well, poor health certainly appears at some point. Dissatisfaction with ourselves and with our lives will appear too. Resentment and frustration can take over. We might blame others for what we perceive as something we lack. Finding fault everywhere is a major clue that a burnout is ahead. Please observe your own life and be honest. Is this occurring for you?

Quiet, inward reflection is necessary for a rich, rewarding, moment-to-moment life. We can find the time, we can take the time, and we can make the effort. It doesn't have to be long, but it is helpful if it is often. I have a young friend who was doing seven hours of spiritual practice a day when I first met her. A few years later, she said that a ten-minute meditation was more productive than the seven hours was before.

Are our lives about being busy and staying productive? Is that our goal? If so, I suggest we rethink it.

Practice silence as often as you can. Sit and drink a cup of tea without doing anything else. I wrote my wife recently, "Waiting for a client and loving you." She wrote me back, "Multitasking." Her subtle humor shows the depth of her quiet. We need to program quiet time into our calendars. Try being silent at home, even if you live with others. Watch the breath. Be with a few breaths. Feel into the inner landscape.

Seclusion—actively keeping away from others—is necessary for inner well-being. Overcoming the difficulty in doing it, is the cost that we pay, to find true inner peace.

Significance: Sun in Virgo, development, self-discovery, wasting time, worrying, vanity, complaining, stillness, clarity, resilience, clear direction, diligence, living in the moment

Lessons: We all long for outward success, prosperity, and recognition. The 8 of Gravity shares that working on ourselves may speed up our pursuit of these goals. With diligence and quiet, we can save ourselves from false starts and missteps.

Practices: Are there aspects of being alone that are unsettling to you? Can you find the place inside where you overcome your challenges? How would it feel to have a whole weekend to be still and quiet by yourself?

Next Step: Schedule some downtime for personal rejuvenation and exploration.

Contemplate: I am happiest when I am free and have the simplest of needs.

Higher Octave: I meet myself in the quiet of aloneness.

Affirmation: I relax and trust in the higher Self.

9 of GRAVITY

I have always enjoyed Islamic art and its use of geometric designs in architecture. The geometric patterns reflect a sense of unity and order present at all times, while giving the artist the ability to express freely and with flexibility. The Muslim artist isn't attempting to replicate nature. Instead, the focus is on reflecting life and the greatness of creation. Geometry is very spiritual. Circles have no end and represent infinity in nature as well as the infiniteness of God or Allah. I find the designs exhilarating and uplifting. They mesmerize me. The sense of expansion allows me to feel all possibilities.

Experience: Creativity and Genius

I find it interesting that outside creative forces can inspire our creativity. When I'm feeling unwell, or in a creative slump, I'm often re-inspired by music, a book, or a movie. Life can inspire as well. Meeting people and having experiences is uplifting. Simply living life encourages creativity. These external forces stimulate my own juices. It is like a hormone or protein rush. How does this work for you? The same way?

One musician I enjoy and respect is Elton John. Elton taught himself to play the piano at four years old, and he has worked with his collaborator, Bernie Taupin, for over fifty years. Bernie writes the words; Elton puts them to music. When they prepare to make a new album, they get together beforehand so Elton can lay out a theme or mood for the album. Then, Bernie goes off and writes poems. Once the poems are done, Elton goes to the studio and quickly writes the songs.

One of the most amazing things about how Elton works is the speed at which he writes songs. It is said that it only took him twenty minutes to write "Tiny Dancer." How can this be?! He allows himself to get into the rhythmic flow of it. This process isn't accomplished with his mind. He feels the lyrics, and then his hands know what to play to express those feelings. There is no questioning or doubting—it's a forward-facing process. He does not shrink back from the writing of the song. Instead, he fully goes for it. It's genius.

But this theme isn't about Elton or me. The theme is about you. It's about creativity and genius. Genius comes in many different forms. There's genius in the flow of creativity. There's genius in having skilled talent plus expression. It is available to all of us.

There is a life to creativity—a spark, a flame, a vibrancy, a vitality. And it isn't unique to creativity, so if we are not feeling creative, we can still experience the same vitality in love, generosity, empathy, nature, and in thousands of actions and feelings available to humanity. What is special about creativity is the growth that happens—making something new, connecting ideas and things in new ways. It makes life endlessly interesting and fulfilling. Creativity overcomes obstructions and turns roadblocks into opportunities. By using our own genius, we gain new perceptions at the core of our creative moments.

Significance: Venus in Virgo, integrity, self-confidence, gain, success, attainment, intuition, uncertainty, doubt, judgments, comparisons, self-righteousness, anxiety, independence, love

Lessons: Consistent effort results in significant gains in important areas. The 9 of Gravity reminds us how gratitude keeps us from foolish, unwise actions when we ignore inner wisdom. The purity of our engagements keeps us on the path to freedom.

Practices: How do you feel creativity? How do you get inspired? Do you have personal catalysts?

Next Step: Be grounded in gravity and open to flow.

Contemplate: The uplifting beauty in the world.

Higher Octave: The greater the will, the greater the flow of energy.

Affirmation: I feel joy expressing from my heart.

10 of GRAVITY

The tree of life grows from the feminine body in a kind of primordial, mystical space of mindfulness, grounding, and connection between mind, body, and Spirit. Her body is supported by magnificent roots as she is intertwined with the growth of the tree. She is Mother to all, offering her body in service. I honor the role and the expression, as I honor the feminine in each being.

Experience: Divine Feminine

Most people in the West—men and women—are tuned to their masculine energy and qualities. The hectic, achievement-based Western society doesn't value masculine and feminine energies equally, so feminine energy and qualities are less understood and respected.

The divine feminine is important to both men and women, and respecting it aids our awakening.

Divine feminine is not female. It is a polar energy to masculine energy—a flavor, as it were. Every aspect of life has positive and negative pole qualities. To fully express, live, and manifest, we need to include vibrations that contain all. Male energy needs feminine sensitivity. Female energy needs masculine assertion. To live at our highest, we need to address and be all the energies.

Here are eight feminine qualities that I believe help express the nourishing feminine being. We grow by spending time reflecting upon them. These qualities germinate into powerful gifts.

Thoughtfulness focuses on being considerate and conscious of other perspectives. The thoughts are not with the *self*. Instead, the *self* diminishes a little in position to others, but not in the sense of self-denial or low self-esteem.

Beauty isn't about outward attraction. There is an inward glow that we recognize as beautiful in an energetic way. Beauty has a sensitivity to it. It has elegance, simplicity, and balance. Beauty is an inward peace beyond any surface distractions.

Empathy is softness and connection towards all of life. It has a non-physical touch. It surrounds and unites through grace and trust in higher truth. Empathy is whole—it surrounds and unites.

Vulnerability lifts the armor of denial and protection. Freedom is at its core. There is nothing to protect when we allow ourselves to feel and express our honest truths. The real *self* needs no protection. We protect ego unnecessarily.

Intuition is openness to the moment. It is empty of our minds, our stories, and our fears. Intuition is listening to the beating heart of the Universe, which can call to us softly even in the middle of the night. Intuition is the inner *knowing*—clear, decisive, and assured.

Patience asks us to give up our own sense of time and timing. It is respect—being, not doing—and is rooted in trust of the Universe. Patience is a good friend to hang out with.

Sensuality puts its best foot forward. It is an assured fullness without measure of other, anything outside the self. It speaks of knowing without any questions. It asks nothing and is without concern for limiting ideas.

Radiance is a fundamental law in nature. Everything radiates. But this radiance has maturity and confidence in its aura. Radiance beams out to others without thoughts of its own. It is a sharing, not a giving away. Radiance gives back to that which has already been provided.

To increase the feminine nature, take in these qualities. Be patient; don't rush them. For like the fruit of the harvest season, they need time to develop and mature into their full flavor. The goal of living consciously will bear fruit when we attend to these divine feminine qualities with effort and sensitivity.

Significance: Mercury in Virgo, fulfilment, completion, stability, inheritance, security, balance, strength, inner wealth, discord, caution, insecurity, doubt, fear, legacy, family

Lessons: The last card is not the end of the journey. The 10 of Gravity reminds us that to enjoy the richness of life, we must touch and share all parts of life by being open with confidence. Holding back may bring stagnation and block energies on spiritual, emotional, and physical levels.

Practices: Which of the qualities mentioned above is your strength? Which of them is a weakness? Come into full flower by working on all of them.

Next Step: Appreciate all that you have.

Contemplate: Life is a book ready to be written.

Higher Octave: I am rich and free in every way.

Affirmation: I surrender all that doesn't serve my highest good.

THE NEXT STEP

We have come to the end of the book. There are no more cards or themes. But I hope this is a beginning, not an ending. We are at a great threshold. The doors are wide open. The opportunities of a lifetime are awaiting your next steps.

Below, I am offering some final thoughts that may be helpful in learning to successfully negotiate life and embrace the open doors that are offered. Living these helpful practices can make a huge difference in how we feel and, frankly, what happens or doesn't happen in life.

Like we ask for abundance but block it with the thought that we don't have what we want, these practices will enhance all aspects of being and can lead to a harmonious, conscious, awakened life. They are helpful for whichever level you are at and whichever level you hope to discover.

Be easy on yourself.

I meet a lot of people who express an amazing amount of compassion for other people, animals in need, and plants that are suffering. They are so sensitive and sincere in caring about all other living beings. But quite often, the person they treat the harshest—and show the least compassion to—is themselves. We need to remember to practice loving ourselves, too. We have what we need at all moments—someone who wants to be loved, appreciated, and shown sympathy. When we practice on ourselves, It's a win-win.

It's a marathon, not a sprint.

It's easy to be calcified against life, assuming the attitude that hard situations won't change. Like when you were a child and you were so upset that your parents wouldn't let you do what you wanted. But can you remember what it was that they wouldn't let you do or have? Does it still bother you? Hopefully, you laugh about it now, maybe with your parents.

When we're in the middle of a challenge, it can seem insurmountable. Your children won't listen to you. Your boss or employees just don't get it. What to do? When we can take a step back, when we let the healing forces oxygenate our blood with a few deep breaths, life can change, simply because we gain a different viewpoint. Life offers so many twists and turns. Friends become enemies. Enemies become friends. Things we never thought we would do become favorite hobbies. When we can take a long-term view of anything, healing is already happening.

Doing it alone is not possible, and yet we do it alone.

What would life be like without other people? People add to our lives in unlimited kinds of ways. On the physical level, the functions are as unique as the number of people we see: helping, serving, transporting, friends, teachers. We eat with them in restaurants. Many give us a helping hand at the ideal moment. Some may push us in line at the grocery

269

store. Sometimes it's nice to take a weekend alone or maybe retreat for a whole week by ourselves, but for most of us, life cannot be lived, enjoyed, and appreciated without the involvement of others.

On a deeper level, others offer us a mirror—they reflect us back to ourselves. It's the gift that never stops giving. Through others, we gain insight into how we are and what we are doing. Often, we can't see these things on our own. The insights blow away the fog that surrounds our lives. All we need to do is be open to the feedback.

That's where our part comes in. No one can think for us, no one can change our attitudes for us. They can make suggestions, and they can hand us medicine, but we have to act and swallow the medicine on our own. We have to face our fears on our own. We have to be the ones to control our anger. We are the only ones who can enable us to stop being arrogant, unworthy, and captive to the myriads of human ignorance that goes through us in a lifetime. So yes, we can't do it alone, yet we do it alone.

Spend time in observation.

It's easy for some of us to react and overreact to circumstances in our life. However, in the heat of a situation, we don't have a clear vision of anything. There is much to be gained by taking time to observe and gain perspective. I seem to remember there was a saying about counting to ten before acting on your anger. I suggest trying a thousand or a million. Watch yourself, study your reactions, reflect on your role, and how people's reactions make you feel. Do this for all big emotions. All situations are lessons, and we benefit from them by studying ourselves. Conscious observation offers the essence of life on a silver platter.

What you eat and how you eat make a difference in how you feel and act.

Our senses are working on our behalf 24/7. The amount of input we ingest is mind-boggling. Both science and spirituality have studied the negative effects our bad habits, tense thinking, and resentments have on our bodies. So many of the mysterious illnesses that society is dealing with have complex causes from a combination of environmental, psychological, and modern life stressors. Modern pharmaceuticals can cause more negative effects than healing.

This is why what we eat is so important. We take in food to nourish the body, to provide the resources it needs for good maintenance, and to replenish it. To eat healthy food in a conscious way, with a positive attitude, is a good step towards whole body health, peace, and contentment. This goes for more than just food. Thoughts, attitudes, media, interactions, vibrations, teachings, emotions, conditioning, and fear can have negative and positive effects on our well-being on all levels. We also take them in. Choose wisely.

Schedule relaxation and fun into your life regularly.

The pace of modern life is not natural, nor is it health-inducing. How is it possible to sit in our wisdom when we are not calm enough to be able to listen clearly? When we don't give ourselves the time we need to recharge our body and soul and discharge stress and agitation, there's a compounding effect. For a while, we can dodge the consequences of unhealthful choices, but when we get older, we pay up. Doctor's visits, pain and suffering, doubting, insomnia—the list goes on and on. Give the gift of life to your being. Take in all your life can offer, sit back in celebration and gratitude for what has been accomplished. Feel into the expansiveness around you. Take the trip, spend a day resting beneath a tree, watch fish jump in a lake, sip your tea while you watch the sunrise. These are wonderful ways to grow and deepen.

Quiet the noise.

I've been fortunate in the last years to spend quite a bit of time out of the United States for months at a time. Upon my return, I'm always overwhelmed by how loud and demanding the culture is in the U.S. From the constant marketing to the intensity of the lifestyle, and the sheer number of choices offered, a sane person is seriously challenged to maintain their center while being pulled in all directions at once. It's easy to give the noise a negative connotation, but it's also an opportunity to see how we react to each moment in the cold light of day. Try keeping to yourself when the noise gets loud. Use discernment in public places so as not to lose your peace and center.

We have too many choices in our lives. As we generally don't discriminate too well, it is easy to get distracted by all the options. Life is an all-you-can-eat buffet from which we gain pounds and indigestion. "Too much" as a lifestyle takes us away from our *self*, rather than helping us find it. That bucket containing our cherished bucket list can develop a hole. *What do I want most? What brings me the most joy and pleasure?* When we are willing to take some time to explore questions like these, then more of our being will participate in whatever we do.

Be aware of what you surround yourself with.

One of my teachers in this life, the famous Indian master, Paramahansa Yogananda, was always quoted as saying, "Environment is stronger than willpower." It's easiest to develop new attitudes and abilities when you are around people who display and inspire those same attitudes. I find writing easier when I hang around words, whether written or spoken (it doesn't seem to matter). Words seem to flow better from words. There are so many negative influences in our greater society. Many are happy to pull us onto their train, not caring whether we want to be a passenger or not. When we bring awareness and discernment to our environments, we will find ourselves living more consciously and uplifted.

We have everything we need, except maybe time.

We spend a lot of our lives searching. A new shampoo, our next trip, a new phone—all can appear important until we experience them. While living life certainly includes enjoying what is possible, the drive to experience it all, seemingly at once, is destructive to our peace of mind. We have everything we need when we *know* that we have it. I sit here wondering what is missing in this universe of "stuff." The only thing I can come up with is "time," but even that is penetrable.

Learn to trust yourself.

Many people find it hard to trust the Universe, as if the Universe needs our trust to work. How can we trust something or someone we don't know? Let me turn that question around. How can we live without trusting? Not very well. I live with trust because living without trust is too painful. If I allow fear to guide my actions, how can I know where the line is between fear and trust? Who will remind me to get off the fear express train? When we feel trust within, we can trust anyone and everything. Trust means letting go of expectations about results. I trust all to do the best they can, including myself. I trust that everything unfolds without needing to place a value of "good," "bad," or "scary" onto it.

Learn to recognize when the seesaw tips.

We can work on inner growth issues for a long time before we see the results we aspire to attain. We can become very impatient waiting for the right moment. There is a point when the courage needed for the change and the determination to show up for oneself becomes greater than the desire to stay small and live limited by fear and anger. There's a point when the seesaw tips, we see life differently, and growth will come almost effortlessly, because we have released the blocks keeping us from our emergence. Learn to recognize that the seesaw doesn't tip when we have weighed down one end with our patterned behaviors. When we release them and cultivate new, lighter actions, the seesaw will tip, and we will have passed through another dharma door—a lesson of life. We can will every seesaw to tip, by right action, best attitude, and releasing the blocks.

Be your own best friend.

We look outside ourselves to satisfy all our desires and needs. Our culture reinforces the idea that we are not complete without the items it has for sale. Wherever we go, the message is the same: something is lacking, and what fills that lack is just around the corner. Forever looking forward, it's no surprise that we stub our toes. Who among our friends and acquaintances will step forward to say you are complete and beautiful the way you are? The friendship we need to develop is the one with the true *self*. Be your own best friend. Support yourself, be compassionate to yourself, and complement yourself with the gift of love. This is a gift that never stops giving. Be objective with yourself. It's okay to find things you want to change. But when we live in acknowledgement that we do the best we can, even if we *can* do better, we become our own best friend.

COMING HOME

Ultimately, coming home means living in complete integrity. It means always living in one's *truth*. It is also living in the moment—not in the past or future, not in emotions, not in mental ideas, not in conditioned behavior, not in childhood ways of being.

For most people, it takes a long time—many adult decades—to discover these truths. There are many levels to this discovery, which serves as a path rather than an end achievement.

Indra's Net is meant to be relevant to readers at all levels of experience. All of us experience new levels of coming home over our lifetimes.

But at each stage, we can come home to a sense of *self.*

Like coming to integrity.

Like coming to self-assurance.

Like coming to liking ourselves.

Like coming to peace about the stage of life we are in.

Like coming to acceptance of our family, both as a child and a parent.

Like coming to joy about what we have and haven't done in life.

Like coming to accept flow.

Like coming to release our hurt from others and life.

Like coming to see that life isn't scary all the time.

Like coming to see that truth is possible.

Like coming to live with self-worthiness.

Like coming to release body tension.

This is the method of how *Indra's Net* brings us home. No good, no bad, no shame, no curse, no stuck, no doom, no rigid way of living with no way out.

In each moment, all possibilities exist, and we can live in light and love, which are always around us. It's a process of alignment—discovery, not becoming. With alignment, we open to wisdom—consciousness. It's like sound healing, which tunes us to healing frequencies. We don't know, then we open up; we align; then we know.

ACKNOWLEDGEMENTS

I've grown and matured from my interactions with *Indra's Net*. I feel full and complete, for it has taught me on every level. My prayer is that it will do the same for you, for here we are, God serving God.

Thank you to Marianne for her unending love and support. Her beauty touches many of these pages. Books are team efforts: special thanks to Krista Huber, who was instrumental in making the book a reality. I will always appreciate her commitment and vision for the book. Thanks to Laura Thomas for her empowering editing. Thanks to Kimberly Mangino and Paul Green for tremendous early support and insights. Thanks to Jennifer McEuen for the amazing cover art. Thanks to Stephen Sturgess, Teja Watson, and Yoshiko Prema Swan for their contributions. Unending gratitude to my parents, long gone from this Earth, who inspired a deep love of books in me at an early age, and allowed the seeds of my adventurous mind to germinate.

To the multitude of nameless, faceless people who grace these pages, who aren't nameless or faceless to me, thanks for sharing the experiences of life and for touching my heart deeply. Much gratitude to Tarot for its innate wisdom and huge Spirit. Deepest soul felt appreciation and wonderment to God and Guru for the never-ending grace and guidance.

ABOUT THE AUTHOR

Indra Rinzler is a lifetime spiritual seeker and has been studying astrology and spirituality for more than 50 years. As a culmination of his life's work, he offers life readings for clients using Vedic astrology, the Enneagram of Personality, Astrocartography, and the Wheel of Totality. In his work, he aims to help people live in the moment, beyond their conditioned stories.

As a world traveler of more than 25 years, he lives most of the year in the foothills of Northern California, and spends his winters in India. Aside from his readings, he writes, teaches, heals, and counsels, and is a frequent guest on podcasts. *Indra's Net* is his first book. You can learn more about him and his work at IndraRinzler.com

www.ingramcontent.com/pod-product-compliance
Lightning Source LLC
Chambersburg PA
CBHW080900120626
46555CB00008B/2894